• • • • • • • • •

New Directions
in Career Planning
and the Workplace

New Directions in Career Planning and the Workplace

• • • • • • • • •

PRACTICAL STRATEGIES FOR COUNSELORS

Jean M. Kummerow, Editor
With an Introduction by Ron Visconti

·D|B· Davies-Black Publishing
Palo Alto, California

Published by Davies-Black, a division of Consulting Psychologists Press, Inc., 3803 E. Bayshore Road, Palo Alto, California 94303, 1-800-624-1765.

99 98 97   10 9 8
Printed in the United States of America

Library of Congress Cataloging-in-Publication Data
New directions in career planning and the workplace : practical strategies
    for counselors / Jean M. Kummerow, editor, with an introduction by
    Ron Visconti.
        p.   cm.
    Includes bibliographical references.
    ISBN 0-89106-050-2
    1. Career development. 2. Vocational guidance. I. Kummerow, Jean M.
HF5549. 5. C35N48   1991
658.3--dc20   91-18206
                                                                        CIP
First edition
    First printing 1991

Contents

II New Directions in the Workplace

• • • • • • • • • •

Introduction

The contemporary work environment is in a constant state of flux. The 1980s were characterized by unprecedented change, including mergers and acquisitions, technological change, the globalization of the marketplace, and changing demographics, resulting in an increasingly multiethnic work force. All indicators suggest that the 1990s will be just as volatile, if not more so.

The climate of change is not only external, but internal—that is, within those who are seeking careers. People change careers more frequently than ever before, and they are demanding more satisfaction in terms of what they do, where they do it, who they do it with, and how they execute their job duties. A career decision is no longer just one of getting a job and moving up in the company; it is an integral part of the total life experience and growth of the individual.

The fluctuations in the work environment, together with the high expectations of career seekers, make career development more complex than ever before. It also requires that both counselors and clients stay abreast of trends in employment as well as world events that may affect one's employment.

In addition, individuals need to know more about themselves and about their options in terms of work styles. For example, does one go into business for oneself or work in a corporate setting? Is consulting an option?

Is working at home or job sharing a viable solution to meet the challenge of balancing one's home and career lives?

Technology is constantly changing. Shorthand is virtually obsolete and word processing and computer literacy prerequisites now for most clerical jobs. Changes occur so rapidly that individuals are constantly having to upgrade their skills just to keep up with the current work requirements. This trend is evidenced by the burgeoning training industry.

Traditional roles for men and women have changed. Most women, whether or not they are married or have children, work outside the home for a large percentage of their lives. The work force increasingly comprises nonwhite employees and women. Women are not content with the jobs previously seen as "women's occupations"—clerical work, nursing, teaching, domestic service, and waitressing. They are now managers, doctors, lawyers, and tradespeople. And some men, weary of the corporate rat race, are choosing to pursue their own businesses or stay home and raise children, at least for a given time period.

Job security is no longer the norm. With the constantly changing workplace come layoffs and relocations and all the accompanying stress. Some people are experiencing a shorter workweek, more leisure time, and early retirement. Some employers are creating part-time or job-sharing positions and offering such options as flextime or working at home. All this creates the need for people to make more and more decisions about their employment. And decision making requires increased information about oneself and options for employment. Choosing a job can be proportionately as complex as choosing from an expanded selection of ice cream from three to thirty-one or more flavors!

As career counselors, we must be ever aware of the trends and forecasts that we can use to help our clients make informed choices. How do we present all the options available to our clients? What skills will our clients need to keep up with the market demands? How do we prepare our clients to examine the larger life issues that will affect their career decisions? How can we help our clients to acquire the research skills they will need to help themselves continue the lifelong career development process?

As career counselors, we need to see the whole picture yet recognize the uniqueness of each individual and to balance trends with each individual's personal skills and needs. For example, if an individual were really gifted as a musician and the market did not indicate a high need for musicians, should we discourage the individual from pursuing a career in music? No, we must find ways to help the individual find a career in music despite the scarcity of possibilities.

As individuals, we will probably be forced to make several career decisions in our lives. The chances of our finding employment in our twenties and remaining on the same job until retirement are very slim.

Whether or not we seek career guidance from the outside, we will need to learn how to change careers, make the most informed decisions, and know ourselves as we evolve along with our careers. Counselors will need to gear their work toward this reality.

This anthology is designed to help us raise our consciousness, to help us think about our roles as counselors so that we can implement our skills more effectively and create a dynamic process between our clients and ourselves.

Experts in a variety of fields have been chosen to collaborate on this volume, specifically, such experts as Mark Guterman, Dennis Jaffe, Jean Kummerow, Rick Mirabile, Andrea Saveri, Cynthia Scott, Judith Waterman, and Dave Wigglesworth. Topics discussed include the multiethnic work force, career pathing, balancing of home life with careers, job trends, and career assessment.

I would like to acknowledge the countless hours of work and coordination that went into the production of this anthology. We hope that you will find this book helpful in assisting you, the counselor, with your task of preparing your clients for an ever-changing workplace.

Ron Visconti
July 1991

Preface

• • • • • • • • •

I have a confession to make as a professional in the field of career development—I don't like to even think about my own career, let alone plan it. I just like to let it happen, and I always end up doing interesting things. In fact, that's how I ended up editing this book. Lee Langhammer Law of Consulting Psychologists Press called and asked if I would take over the project. The original editor could unfortunately no longer carry through, but the project was worth continuing. What an interesting road this book has led me down with the opportunity to work with some great ideas and some great authors.

There are already many good books available on career development and counseling. What this one adds is its concise descriptions of many of the trends in the field—continual adjustment of our directions, dealing with change, labor force patterns, testing, competency identification, multicultural dimensions, and dual careers. Additionally, this book goes a bit further by making many practical suggestions on how you can use your knowledge of the issues to help your clients in their own career development. This book has something for everyone in the field with its focus on new directions in career planning and in the workplace.

The first section focuses on career planning. "Career and Life Planning: A Personal Gyroscope in Times of Change" by Judith A. Waterman introduces us to the powerful image of the gyroscope guiding our way through our own career and life changes. She pulls together many of the elements of the field, highlighting theoretical contributions and personal applications. We find there are always adjustments to make in the career development process and with the help of this chapter we can get on course.

The second chapter, "Career Development for Empowerment in a Changing Work World" by Dennis T. Jaffe and Cynthia D. Scott, succinctly identifies many of the changes we've been feeling in the workplace and even defines the new issues. It includes a highly practical and useful workbook to explain the concept of career development and to guide clients through the five stages of that process.

The third chapter, "Using the *Strong Interest Inventory* and the *Myers-Briggs Type Indicator*® Together in Career Counseling" by Jean M. Kummerow, moves us into a specific aspect of career counseling—the use of tests—with a focus on the highly popular and widely used *Strong* and MBTI. Combining these tests gives even more to both the client and the career counselor. Jaffe and Scott's stages are incorporated with specific suggestions on how to use the instruments in each.

"Competency Profiling: A New Model for Career Counselors" by Richard J. Mirabile invites us to look at another aspect of careers, mainly job competencies. He provides persuasive arguments regarding the importance of the job/person match on knowledge, skills, and abilities and offers suggestions for getting started on this process.

Our next section focuses on the changes in the workplace, beginning with an excellent overview by Andrea Saveri in "The Realignment of Workers and Work in the 1990s." The complex changes in our work force, including its diversification and aging, are explained clearly and simply, with many helpful suggestions for us to use in our work. Changes in occupational trends are also forecast and the implications of those presented. You'll find statistical data explained with much clarity.

The sixth chapter, "Meeting the Needs of the Multicultural Work Force" by David C. Wigglesworth, continues the increasingly important diversity theme and expands it to the multicultural world in which we live and work. Issues are identified and strategies to work with diversity are presented.

Finally, the book ends with "Working Couples: Finding a Balance Between Family and Career" by Mark Guterman. Anyone in a dual career relationship will find something helpful in this chapter. The issues for individuals, organizations, and career counselors are clearly outlined and many suggestions given to deal with the pressures faced.

So while I began with a confession, let me end with one also. This editing process has been a worthwhile one for me. After many years in the field, I now feel even better informed and even more comfortable with my own directions. Thanks to Judy, Dennis, Cynthia, Rick, Andrea, Dave, Mark, and Lee for your contributions to me and to this book.

Jean M. Kummerow, Ph.D.
July 1991

I

· · · · · · · · ·

New Directions
in Career Planning

1

• • • • • • • • •

Career and Life Planning:
A Personal Gyroscope in Times of Change

JUDITH A. WATERMAN

Career counseling is often perceived as a onetime event, a step toward making a single, major job change. But as the Greek philosopher Heraclitus argued around 400 B.C., nothing endures but change. It's a pervasive truth; internal and external forces bring constant change to our careers and to personal lives, each of which is inextricably bound to the other.

Good career counseling, then, is more than assisting a client through a single work-related passage. Done right, it can prepare and guide an individual through a lifetime of change. Done well, it could be a means to manage the twists, dilemmas, and quandaries that nearly everyone faces at one time or another. It is a permanent personal gyroscope that career counselors and their clients can use to keep on target in times of change.

A *gyroscope* is defined as a device used "to maintain equilibrium and determine direction."[1] And that is precisely what good career and life planning can do as we face personal life, career, and individual changes.

Consider Phil's plight, Margo's dilemma, and Bill's quandary:

▶ Phil Stockton had lived in the Denver area his entire life. After high school, he attended the University of Colorado at Boulder and earned a degree in chemical engineering. He spent a year with a government research lab, returned to Boulder for his MBA, and then joined a major telecommunications firm. Meanwhile, he married Sue, a high school English teacher whom he had dated since their sophomore year in college. They both liked to hike and ski, so most weekends found them heading for the nearby mountains. The couple purchased a home in Englewood, a Denver suburb, and within a few years had two children. Stockton's ties to the region were deep indeed.

A midlevel manager, Stockton felt comfortable with his career until his firm was taken over by a larger company. The culture and political climate shifted toward bureaucracy and a system that seemed to favor parent company employees and new hires. On decisions important to his work, Stockton was increasingly out of the loop. His discontent festered and grew.

Through a cousin, Phil heard that a small telecommunications company in Atlanta wanted someone with his background. While he thought it unlikely that he'd be offered the job, he discussed it with Sue. The two agreed he should apply, primarily for the interviewing practice. However, the Atlanta company responded and persisted for four flattering months. It then offered him a job with more responsibility and at a better salary than his current position.

It was a wish granted, the solution to a situation that was making Stockton miserable, but with it came a host of thorny dilemmas. Sue had a good teaching position in Englewood. With friends and relatives nearby, child care was never a problem. Unlike the old job, the new one involved travel. And Atlanta is a long way from Colorado's ski slopes. What should Phil do?

▶ Margo Crystal was a savvy 23-year-old with a quick and easygoing laugh, but with a serious personality and determination to find a rewarding career. After graduating with honors from Dartmouth, she and several friends traveled through Europe for six months. At the end of her trip, Margo found work as a salesperson in a London department store. That job quickly proved uninteresting, so she found another, this time writing internal communications for a chain of retail stores. All too soon, however, Margo began to feel she was going nowhere professionally.

"I want a career, not a job," she told a career counselor upon returning to the United States. "I see my friends jump from one job to another. I even started my working life that way. But that's not what I want. The next company I join should be for a long time. I also want to work up quickly to some real responsibility."

Margo wanted to make a commitment. But she had no clear idea of the kind of position, company, or even industry to approach. Since she seemed intent on wedding her work life to the first offer that seemed right, could she be on risky ground?

▶ Bill Kaible, an attractive, fit-looking 42-year-old, had just lost his job with the corporate law department of an international transportation company. He'd seen the corporate problems that led to the downsizing coming but figured it would never affect him. Despite a severance package that included four months of salary, he was angry, frustrated, and frightened.

He was also alone. During the past three years, tensions had built up at home between Kaible and his wife, stress that likely caused him to ignore the problems at work. Were it not for his two sons, ages 8 and 13, he'd have filed for divorce sooner. Now he was in the middle of divorce proceedings and without a job.

However, at times Kaible felt the fear and anger give way to a feeling of renewal. "My marriage was filled with so much friction," he told a career counselor. "And as far as work goes, I haven't really liked law since about a year after I got out of law school. I think I went into law because so many of my friends did. I'll admit that it's scary looking for a job for the first time in nearly 20 years. But this is my chance to start over, and I want some happiness out of life."

Career-Life Dilemmas

Clearly, Phil, Margo, and Bill were all in the midst of career and life changes. They were not just considering their jobs, but their lifestyles as well. For good career planning then, counselor and client must examine both personal and career realities and objectives.

If we look at only the career side of Phil Stockton's plight, most people in a job search would say, What's his problem? He's got a great job offer and never really had to go job hunting. But Phil is a disheartened man. Taking the job in Atlanta could cause far more problems than it solves.

Margo had little experience or information on which to base any decisions. She faced choosing her first "serious" job and saw it as a direct path to an ultimate or lifelong career. But she needed to understand that most new graduates will change jobs an average of ten times in a lifetime, with an average of four or five careers in often unrelated fields. It's virtually certain that the job market and she too will change; understanding these few facts can greatly influence choices made today.

Out of seeming disaster, Bill Kaible perceived a bright opportunity for change. While optimistic, he nonetheless feared that within two years of starting a new career, he'd grow bored and develop the same distaste he had for law. With his home life in shambles, Bill was in the midst of major change.

What all three needed was a way to respond to the changes they faced, a plan of sorts, but one that also is a map, an information base, a checkpoint, and even a source of reinspiration. Such a technique doesn't aim and propel one straight toward the ultimate target, like an arrow from a bow. Instead the technique can be likened to a gyroscope keeping a rocket aimed at a moving target, checking and rechecking its trajectory, continually assessing direction, making corrections, and altering direction as events unfold. Good career and life planning can be a guide that helps one make choices; it is most powerful if created before a choice must be made.

Later in the chapter we'll return to Phil, Margo, and Bill and how they coped. Meanwhile let's look first at the various possible axes of the gyroscope, then pull a working model together.

The Initial Choice

A few fortunate people seem to make the right initial job choice; most don't. For better or worse, outside influences and luck, rather than forethought or planning, normally guide their selection.

In the 1970s, the electronics industry and the action in Northern California's Silicon Valley had a tremendous allure for college graduates. In the superheated financial climate of the 1980s, venture capital, investment banking, and management consulting promised six-figure salaries and a seemingly limitless future. In the 1990s, law is emerging more than ever as a popular career choice. While each of these were, and perhaps still are, financially and socially rewarding careers, many young people choose them for the wrong or inappropriate reasons—from availability to pack-following behavior.

Perhaps the first influence on career paths is a parental model, followed by other personal role models such as teachers, adult friends, and even the media. A friend, teacher, or school counselor may recognize a certain talent—for example, in music, computer programming, or organization—and encourage a career in that direction. Geography also plays a role, such as the proximity to Boeing for college graduates in Washington state. Gaining recognition for running the fastest, earning the best French grades, or landing the lead in the class play further lures some to related fields.

There are also discouraging factors, some that are self-generated and some that come from others. A skill may come so easily to an individual that he or she thinks everyone can do it, thus giving it little respect and holding scant hope for its future as a profession. Careers that demand exceptional talent and hard work, such as acting, music, and the arts, are often considered risky, flaky, or both. Parents counsel their children to steer away. In the pragmatic vein, the requisite schooling for a specific career may be out of financial reach. While the young can flash self-assurance or rebellion, confidence is often shattered by well-meaning but critical adults.

Wise parents, as well as counselors, will offer information to young people that encourages optimistic exploration of the world and themselves. They will also urge discussions that explore false assumptions. Psychologist Dr. John Krumboltz warns: "People often make assumptions about themselves and the world of work that may or may not be true and have beliefs that could be self-limiting. I could never be an accountant, one might say, or, I'm sure I'd be good at management, when they've never tried it."[2] Unrealistic expectations can lead to poor choices.

Frequently, the expedience of needing a job, any job, compels young people to take whatever they can get. It's the rare person who is fortunate enough to match personal passion and talent to a well-paying vocation from the very beginning. Those who make a great first career choice rarely need career counseling. When they do, it's because the dream sours—say, when the athlete grows too old, the child model grows up, the money gets too tight, or a lifestyle becomes unbearable. Most others make first choices from a limited menu.

Sally Williams, the only child of a Philadelphia physician, exemplifies similar external expectations, and lack of that personal gyroscope, in her initial career choice. Deeply respectful of her father (her mother died when she was 12), Sally wanted desperately to please him and thought that what would most do so was to emulate his career. Although she didn't particularly want to be a doctor, this profound influence led her to what, on the surface, seemed like a highly successful career as a professor of public health. It pleased her father, but left Sally unfulfilled.

Even though her job performance was consistently exceptional, her discontent grew. After seven years, three jobs, many publications and academic accolades, and still unhappy, she approached a career counselor. Following extensive self-assessment, Williams joined a biogenetics firm in marketing and is step-by-step working her way into general management where her heart and true interest really lie.

Career strategist Lili Pratt works with executives in transition as well as with MBA graduates looking into new careers or making an initial job choice. She notes that graduate school training is a very powerful socializer. "Everyone goes into it with their own interests and comes out hoping to work for large consulting firms such as McKinsey and Boston Consulting Group," she explains. "They want to be involved with big corporations, have high visibility, and jump onto a steep learning curve. But in the first 18 months, virtually everyone goes through a metamorphosis. The reality bears little resemblance to what they anticipated—and many are often disappointed."[3] Again, the same pattern—external influence, no internal guidance system, no gyroscope.

When careers are chosen for inappropriate reasons, or when internal or external factors change the conditions, dissatisfaction eventually arises. It may take three years, ten years, or two decades. It's at a point, Pratt says,

> when you see women saying it's time for them to have kids. Would-be entrepreneurs want to start their own company. Some people will stop, take a trip around the world, and come back feeling that they hate everything they've ever done. It's when career counselors run into people who have done some serious soul-searching about what's really important in their lives. Is it family? Is it the children? Is it where they want to live? Or the kind of work they want to do?

> It becomes clear that the career is finally getting put into perspective with the whole picture of their life. They examine whether it's balanced, or out of skew. You see a lot of divorces at this point, lots of babies and little sleep. People really come to grips with it in their own way. What you end up with is a retempered human being.

For a host of reasons people don't get their gyroscopes calibrated at the outset. In an ideal world, we would start the job search with our gyroscopes calibrated and spinning. Career counselors ought to urge more of that. But the world isn't ideal. And for many, a part of the calibration process may, in fact, be trial and error.

Relentless Change

The first job choice is like taking the first step in a long journey. While most people need to do more listening to their own needs at the outset, the more important need is to use continuing change as a way of establishing or keeping on course—not as a continuing set of annoyances that throw us off course. Change is often opportunity in disguise, sometimes, as Winston Churchill said, very well disguised.

Since change cannot be avoided, can we use it to our advantage? Companies merge, downsize, go out of business. New technologies create entirely new industries and put others out to pasture. Environmental factors totally outside a person's control can also force change.

People repeatedly move to new geographic locations—perhaps a dozen times in their lifetimes. They marry and have children. They get divorced. Families combine in remarriages. Kids leave home, sometimes return with their new families in tow, and leave again. Fathers become the primary parent, mothers the traveling executive.

It behooves both the counselor and the client to address such environmental, societal, and industrial trends. Moreover, a counselor must not overlook the fact that the client represents more than him or herself. That person's life influences, and is influenced by, invisible others, as well as by the realities of the world in which he or she lives. Change ripples with the same effects as pebbles thrown in a pond.

Various career experts view change in different ways. While some emphasize the importance of environmental factors, others view it through a lens of life transitions. Some see change as an opportunity to develop wisdom; some stress the disorientation of change, and still others say, Try it and learn from it.

Pat Templin, a career consultant and outplacement specialist, admits that her background in anthropology sways her toward a theory she calls *symbolic interaction*.[4] It tries to explain the forces that various situations and other people exert on a person's life:

> The schools you go to, the companies where you work, your family, your friends—all those influence your expectations about the changes that will occur in your life. They also influence the ways you react to change and when it feels like you need a new pot to grow in. Your perspectives change, your notion of "fit" changes.
>
> There's an interactive quality about people's sense of reality. People's perception of reality is different from situation to situation, so they tend to respond differently in different environments. For that reason, when people are faced with the crisis of changing jobs, they are capable of rising to the occasion and meeting that stress. In the environment of transition, they make more changes than is usually expected of adults.

Said in a different say, many folks rise nicely to uncertainty along the way. They use change to understand themselves better. They build better gyroscopes as they move through time.

Adult education expert Ed Chiosso agrees with the need for a personal guidance system.[5] He argues that change is easiest if people know themselves—and is simpler if they can change the externals *instead* of themselves:

The secret is to find a match between who you are and an environment that suits you. If you want a better job, find a better match. So how can you know what's a good match? The first rule is to know who you are, what you need and want and what your skills are. You may not have to change anything about yourself other than location. And it's sure easier to find a new location than it is to change or adapt. If you can't do that, then you have to adapt. But either way, if you don't know yourself, nothing but luck can help you make those decisions.

Some psychologists view change within the framework of life transitions. They assert that although adult development tends to be slower than child development, there is still an ever-forward process of growth with periods of both stability and transition. In healthy personalities these internal motivations cause people to actively seek new challenges to fulfill their potential. Roger Gould's *Transformations,* Daniel Levinson's *Seasons of a Man's Life,* and George Valliant's *Adaptation to Life* all deal extensively with this issue. Their line of reasoning suggests that there are certain points in most people's lives where the personality makes a conscious adjustment in direction and changes the gyroscope accordingly.

Richard Bolles, author of *What Color Is Your Parachute,* adds a different wrinkle. He argues that stages of life have less to do with change than with whether or not people use change to develop wisdom: "It's a person's experiences that cause them to change," he says. "But an experience always has two parts to it. The first is the actual event, and the second is the person's interpretation and response to the event. The hardest thing to do is take people's attention off what they did wrong, especially when it was a negative experience. You need to make mistakes because that's one powerful way to learn. Positive change occurs as people are able to look at their mistakes and learn from them."[6]

Whatever precipitates or forces change may not particularly matter, nor does it mean that a mistake has been made. While one may grow unhappy in a career after a decade, this does not necessarily mean it was a wrong or totally inappropriate choice. Nor does the choice of a spouse and marriage that ends in a divorce after 15 years mean that the first 12 years and three great kids are disasters. Moreover, there are pieces within these experiences that are critical to synthesizing a career and life planning guide.

David Krantz was at one time a school psychologist and is now in marketing and sales. "I can't think of two more different professions," he muses. "So the question comes up, was one of those the wrong career? Of course there is that possibility, but there's also the distinct possibility that I changed and just needed a new way to develop."[7]

When his children say they don't know what they want to do when they grow up, says Krantz, "I say, 'Neither do I.' I tell them that whatever they do, it's career development, not a career." This is a crucial point. Given the unpredictability of change and the fact that people live longer lives these days, one career plan is seldom sufficient. Nor is simply setting the gyroscope once and forgetting it. The process is calibration and recalibration as life moves on. Counseling at its finest is helping clients develop gyroscopes that can be continually recalibrated—with or without professional help.

Stress may be change's silent partner or its clangorous companion. At times it can scare even the most enthusiastic risk-taker. For those who thrive on stability, it can be terrifying. People often feel disoriented or depressed. They may overvalue the past. They may vacillate in mood as well as progress. Counselors can help clients understand that change, and the stress accompanying it, is normal. They can suggest coping mechanisms such as relaxation techniques or physical exercise to relieve anxiety. It may take some time to reestablish equanimity, but, in this case, patience truly is a virtue.

In their book, *In Search of Excellence*,[8] Peters and Waterman use the phrase, "Ready, fire, aim." They were not arguing against the need for a map, a plan, or a gyroscope. What they were saying is that one of the best ways businesses have of developing that map is to try something and then learn from it. Career planning is similar. Change is relentless; much of life cannot be predicted. However, intelligent use of past experience can be a dominant way to get that gyroscope spinning and vectored.

Past as Prologue

The most dependable place to look for what will motivate people in the future is in their past. What did they especially enjoy learning about, participating in, or doing when they were in school? What have they liked and not liked about their various paid and nonpaid jobs, avocations, and other activities? When we examine such experiences, we discover patterns of motivation that not only existed in their past but reveal clues to what will be fulfilling in their future as well.

Dr. Sally Brew, a former professor turned organizational development specialist, agrees that what motivates people often lurks in patterns from their past. "I believe that people have some built-in mechanism that urges us to strive for new boundaries, but within constraints," she says. "These constraints are patterns that have motivated us in the past and continue to motivate us."[9]

Too frequently, neither the patterns nor the motivations rest at the conscious level. In fact, they can be buried deep in the mind and, in some individuals, are simply ignored. Jim Davidson illustrates just how deeply these things can be buried.

A 29-year-old vice president of a nationally known investment banking firm, Jim Davidson had given little serious thought to his feelings about his career. Guided mainly by what his peers were doing, he easily fell into investment banking after graduating from Princeton.

Davidson spent two years in the securities product division of a New York firm, earned a masters degree from the Yale School of Organization and Management, and proceeded to climb the investment banking ladder. But when the industry went into transition in the mid–1980s, Davidson wanted out. At this point in his life he had no peer group to follow. Although his employer viewed him as a prized talent, Davidson sensed that he had become an "empty suit."

He wasn't an empty person, but he had few clues as to what could be a rewarding career and, sadly, perhaps a fulfilling lifestyle. He began the search for himself with a career counselor. "I want to do something of value, and I don't feel I'm doing that now," he explained. "It can be modest; I don't care. It just has to feel like I'm adding value. I feel stuck, and I don't know how to get unstuck."

Because the clues to the future were so deeply buried, his career counselor feared Davidson might answer test questions in the light of others' identities rather than his own. Thus, she was careful to add additional self-assessment techniques to the battery of tests she assigned. To help him identify the skills he most enjoyed, she assigned Richard Bolles' *Quick Job-Hunting Map,*[10] a lengthy paper-and-pencil exercise. She also used the *System for Identifying Motivated Abilities,*[11] an interviewing technique the roots of which sprout from Bernard Haldane's idea that the clues to personal excellence can be found in our achievements. Both techniques are based on a person's favorite life events and produce profiles that ring true to that person's background.

Davidson was asked to search his past for a number of particularly enjoyable, well-executed experiences. One episode he chose was from childhood when he had helped another eight-year-old boy, Tim, learn to ride a bike. To all outward appearances, Tim seemed not to care about learning to bike, even though that clearly made him something of an outsider in his peer group. But of the whole group, Davidson was the only one who sensed that Tim was covering insecurity. He really wanted to learn but hid his wish behind an "I-don't-care" front. Even at that early age, Davidson's intuitive, caring side was beginning to show.

He also told about how he carefully analyzed, dissected, and reconstructed the steps in learning to ride a bike. Then, intuitively seeing below the nonrider's bravado, Davidson used his analysis to sensitively teach him how to master the skill. Furthermore, being truly helpful and exerting influence in a nonobtrusive way were energizing to Davidson. Other favorite experiences repeated variations of the same attributes that the early bike incident brought to life.

While on the surface Davidson seemed interested in almost everything, including finance, *The Quick Job-Hunting Map* and *System for Identifying Motivated Abilities* suggested other "points of essence." They confirmed that a deeper interest was genuinely contributing to the welfare of others. In addition, they showed his need to combine his analytical problem solving with his intuitive abilities in dealing with people. To achieve a high level of accomplishment and quietly exert influence were also parts of his pattern of skills and motivations.

Thus, Davidson is now concentrating his career search on small service-oriented banks and on for-profit firms that assist the elderly or disadvantaged in their health coverage and financial planning. In this way, he feels he can contribute to the well-being of others while using his well-honed financial skills. (Davidson's natural motivations and skills might well have been fulfilled in academia or social work, but other tests and conversations indicated that he had needs to stay in the private sector.)

Lili Pratt also digs for this essence. "I ask clients to look back over ten years and tell me about the most gratifying thing they ever did," she explains. "And then they can begin to hear what their passion is." That interest or desire may have been part of an original career goal that got sidetracked by practical, make-a-living concerns, family responsibilities, and the like. But it's something a person can return to. Pratt herself is a case in point.

"I was a ballet dancer, and I went into business school with the idea of managing the arts," she says. "I came out as a consultant for Arthur Young." Pratt later joined the Paul Stafford national search firm and became a vice president. "They said a woman couldn't do that, and I did. I needed to be that vice president, and then I woke up and said, So, I have the title. Where's the context? Gosh, this isn't interesting. This is redundant."

So, along with her career consulting and search work, Pratt is involved in fund raising for the ballet. She also takes one weekday off per week for her two children. Her life, while overflowing and overly organized, nevertheless feels balanced.

Pratt's full life is indicative of the subjects that Harrison Gough, the noted psychologist, includes when he extends "past as prologue" to another dimension—that of learning not only from one's own life but from the experiences of others.[12] In particular, he speaks of warning young women about the challenges and solutions of those who walked before. Although many professional and personal problems are shared by men and women, women often face more role and career conflicts, such as balancing a profession and children in periods of limited time and energy.

Dr. Gough believes it is important to bring information on trends revealed by research to a female client's attention. Such data is not meant to limit a woman's expectations, but to help her more clearly see the realities of the world and decide how much she may wish to deviate or comply with its norms.

For years, career development theory ignored women or gave their situation only cursory treatment. However, long overdue research is at last coming forth.[13] Among the findings are some illuminating bits of information. For example:

▶ Women who seek nontraditional roles find it tough, but if the career is right for them and they persevere, difficulties are usually worked through in about 12 years.

▶ Women who have stuck with a pioneering path for approximately 25 years generally achieve a true sense of development and satisfaction.

▶ Women differ from men in the way they react to career progress (as one would normally define it). Research shows that men's personal adjustment usually suffers when they do not move steadily up the career ladder. This is not necessarily true for women. Instead, there is a consistent link between women's effectiveness in their work roles and their overall positive adjustment. Simply put, the research suggests that many women thrive in a rewarding career, without linking happiness and satisfaction exclusively to advancement.

The Value and Hazards of Tests

So far we've talked about several ways of keeping ourselves and our personal career-life gyroscope in alignment. One that we discussed was trying various jobs with the conscious intent of learning from our successes and mistakes. Behaviorist Karl Weick calls this *retrospective sense making* and urges that it is our most powerful tool for navigating the future.[14] Another way we discussed was periodic and rigorous examination of life experiences to learn common patterns of motivation, satisfaction, and dissatisfaction.

A more commonly known way to collect information about ourselves and refine our gyroscopes is through testing. Many people have taken a personality or interest test of some sort. Often, however, they have had at least one bad experience in the process.

The problem is twofold. Some tests, ones we often see in pop magazines, are too simplistic. Other tests, such as the popular *Myers-Briggs Type Indicator* (MBTI)®, have been validated via mountains of research.[15] The problem is that any one test, no matter how valid in general, can seriously misread an individual. A corollary issue is that the prescriptive side of many of these tests is commonly misread by those who do not have a deep understanding of tests, their limitations, their intent, and their strengths.

Printed charts and descriptive explanations from testing companies may make the test seem pat. While these scores and interpretations are excellent discussion guides and give a client later written reference, they often miss valuable subtleties. For instance, on the venerable grandaddy of interest tests, *The Strong Interest Inventory*,[16] results may show that a person has interests similar to those of a funeral director. That certainly doesn't mean one should enroll in embalming classes or send a résumé to every mortuary in the county. But it could, and often does, indicate entrepreneurial interests. A high "funeral director" score most probably means one is disposed to running a small service business or enjoys working with people under stress.

Test results are not always correct. They can vary because people misinterpret or misread several questions, find certain wordings offensive, or answer questions the way they would like to be, rather than the way they are. The point is simple: Career counselors as well as clients should always question the validity of tests. Compare the results of one against others the client has taken. Or relate them to real life experiences. Do they confirm one another? Or do they bring up discrepancies for further investigation? Using just one test is like having only a ruler to measure oranges, footballs, and how much a jar holds.

For instance, one woman felt uneasy with a number of interpretations taken from a lengthy but very inclusive test given in a workshop. When she asked a private career counselor for a second opinion, discussions revealed the probable reason. The morning before the test, she had had a fight with her boyfriend and received a ticket for speeding. Emotional upsets can lead to false test readings. When individuals take a battery of tests scattered over the span of a few days, the chances of faulty results on all of them are greatly reduced.

Both questioning results and combining various scores in and between tests helped Sandra Grey confirm a dream. Then in her mid-thirties, an active volunteer, wife of a doctor, and mother of two teenage boys, she attended a series of small-group career and life planning sessions. Her explicit purpose was to decide whether or not she should attend law school.

Grey's *Strong Interest Inventory* results warned that she might not be "one of the crowd" at law school. Her scores revealed a medium-high interest in the subject of law and politics but very high interests in social service and public speaking. When her interests were compared to those of other lawyers, she scored only moderately high. But when compared to social workers, guidance counselors, speech pathologists, and elected public officials, her scores were very similar.

As the counseling sessions progressed, group discussions only intensified Grey's desire to go to law school. The profession met her image, and she believed it would enable her to contribute to the social good she valued. Guided by her test results, she specialized in a side of law that suited her interests. Today Sandra Grey is a public defender in her home county.

Interests are at the heart of job satisfaction, so career counselors pay special attention to them and rigorously test for them. Consider Al Hammer, now a senior product developer of tests and educational materials. He started off in engineering, received an undergraduate degree in business, got his Ph.D. in counseling, and continually looked for some way to integrate his mathematical, business, and psychological interests. "I'm not sure what urged me to change," he explains. "I think in some ways my interests have always stayed the same, but I've combined them in different ways. I'm also not sure that the interests have changed as much as the opportunities and recognizing that there are other ways to fulfill them."[17] Hammer's point is profound. Core interests for most people remain stable over the years. They provide strong reference points for calibrating that gyroscope.

Tests are designed to ferret out myriad kinds of information. Aptitudes, like interests, are a particularly important fundamental and another dimension of gyroscope calibration. Aptitudes are basic to where we function most comfortably. Because they come naturally and easily, they are a competitive advantage. Aptitudes include such things as small or large muscle coordination and the ability to quickly generate many ideas, see differences in small detail, or visualize three dimensionally. Most professionals agree that aptitudes remain with people throughout their lives—to be called on, developed, and used.

While an experienced counselor can often assess a mature client's aptitudes quite easily, younger people and adults with limited exposure may present a challenge. Sometimes specialists in aptitude testing are the place to turn. For instance, the Johnson O'Connor Research Foundation gives a battery of tests that do an exceptional job in assessing a wide range of innate aptitudes.[18] Astute and responsible counselors may wish to supplement, or even supplant, their own services by recommending such specialists.

But interests temper aptitudes. There are people who can easily perform a skill but aren't interested in using it. While using natural aptitudes gives one a chance to excel, it is far from the only criteria in a career choice.

Byron Steele had chosen a present job three years ago as a result of his Johnson O'Connor aptitude tests. At first he was happy, but soon, no matter how hard he tried to make the job work, he grew less satisfied. Steele visited a career counselor who combined his Johnson O'Connor results with tests and techniques exploring his interests, values, and personality.

The *FIRO-B* (Fundamental Interpersonal Relations Orientation—Behavior),[19] a short, maddeningly repetitive, but amazingly valuable measure of interpersonal behavior, was of particular value to Steele. It revealed a major piece of information that his aptitude tests missed. His FIRO-B scores showed a big discrepancy between the persona he showed others and his inner needs. Outwardly he was friendly, gregarious, and social; inside he was a rather private person. To perform and feel his best, Steele needed a fair amount of time to work and think ideas through on his own. Yet his very friendly manner caused people frequently to stop and chat and even offer collaboration on work that Steele could do (and preferred doing) independently. He felt guilty not responding to their sociable gestures, so the vicious circle and his discontent continued.

He tried to alter his behavior. But impressions are hard to change; his social needs continued to be misinterpreted at his company. Steele grew more frustrated. Finally, he switched to a new firm and moved from product marketing to market research, which more suited his interaction needs and where he is much happier.

Yet another wrinkle in aptitudes is what's sometimes called *multiple intelligences,* a step beyond traditional IQ testing. For too long, intelligence has been primarily equated with verbal and numerical reasoning power, a most narrow view. But people have other kinds of intelligence—mechanical ease, musical genius, artistic flair—and other kinds of natural understandings. These are intelligences of a different sort than get picked up on IQ tests. Exemplified in Howard Gardner's *Frames of Mind* and Robert Steinberg's *The Triarchic Mind,* these new theories demand career counselors' attention.

Other tests and other attributes often carry important clues to career and life satisfaction. An administrative assistant at a shipping firm, Maria Davis sensed that she would enjoy and be good as a manager, although none of her friends or family had ever been in management. Her company had suggested that she consider committing to their management training program, but she hesitated. Davis wanted to be sure that's where she wanted to go.

The *California Personality Inventory* (CPI)[20] proved especially helpful to her. Davis' Dominance score was 76—very high. It revealed that she was assertive, forceful, and self-confident, typically a leader who liked to get things done. Other high scores showed that she had a very strong drive for achievement and was enterprising, dependable, and outgoing. Such characteristics did not surprise Davis; what amazed her was how much higher these scores were than those of most people—how high her need for managing really was.

Personality attributes as strong as Davis' are double-edged swords; they can be a great asset or tremendous weakness. The intensity of her scores told Davis that she needed to use these powerful characteristics. On the other hand, their strength warned that in a management role, she could easily become too dominant and lose the support of her subordinates.

Davis immediately signed into her company's management training program, reenrolled at a local college, and finished her degree in economics. Three years, a marriage, a degree, and a baby later, she is the manager of the same department where she'd served as an administrative assistant.

Career counselors can use tests to help people get personally sensitized to who they are and to winnow down the options to the few things that really count for them. But professionals who use tests must understand their obligations. They must be able to tell clients that the test they've selected is valid for the purposes it's being used.

The *Code of Fair Testing Practices in Education*[21] spells out the major obligations that professionals who develop or use tests have to test takers. While the code is specifically designed for the use of tests in education, it carries excellent guidelines for the use of tests in general.

There are, to be sure, dozens of tests in the career counselor's arsenal. The best compare the subject to *norm groups*, or others in the same age range, sex, or related occupations. Comparing a recent college student to a 20-year work veteran may well be fallacious.

The Elements of a Gyroscope

The reason counselors use tests, self-assessment exercises, and discussions is to discover what's important to a client's success and satisfaction, productivity and happiness. Once all the information is gathered, it's then important to synthesize and simplify it into usable form. Then it can be easily updated and used to evaluate or create alternatives during those inevitable periods of change. The simplified form makes the gyroscope easy to read and to recalibrate.

Three major components help construct this guide, or personal gyroscope. All three influence satisfaction and success for most people. For some, however, one may predominate as a driving force.

▶   *Goals, Wants, and Wishes*—hopes for the future, interests one wants to pursue; in other words what an individual would like to do, have, and be

▶   *Marketable Skills*—what someone will hire us to do in the given economy, considering current trends of employment and technology (i.e., the personal talents, abilities, and qualities for which employers pay good money)

▶ *Personal Yardstick*—personal preferences and characteristics (like personality traits, geographical preferences, financial requisites, prime interests, and natural aptitudes) by which one judges the personal fit of various career directions and choices

Put these three together and one has the major components that constitute a career and life gyroscope. Used with competence, it has the power to direct our course despite external and internal changes. It helps us ask the right questions and look for the right answers.

Goals, Wants, and Wishes

A few folks have no trouble at all articulating goals. Most don't find it that easy. The trouble may relate to the formidable word itself. Goals seems to pertain to lofty and grand aspirations, such as being the president of IBM or winning the Boston Marathon. Aside from saying we want to be happy, most people aren't sure what their grand ambitions should be. For others, "goal" is a specific: I want to retire the December after I am sixty-two, or I want to complete my masters degree in psychology two years after Max begins kindergarten.

It's a different question, however, when a client, equipped with test results and incisive analysis of past experiences, is asked to make a list in which goals include wants, wishes, desires, ambitions, hopes, dreams, ideas, and plans—no matter how fanciful or previously unspoken they might be. Then individuals can usually spin out a long list with ease. The goal set is even easier to construct when such desires are placed in categories such as health/fitness, mental/intellectual, social interaction, special relationships, work/careers, and the like. Thinking in multiple categories can stimulate and expand ideas about a person's desires in life.

Of course, where one wants to live can sometimes dominate other desires. Property managers in San Jose, California, move to Lake Tahoe and pursue the same job in order to ski or hike regularly. Some people work at jobs in which they have minimal interest just to live where they want. Ardent surfers drive taxis just to be in Honolulu. Aspiring actors wait tables to live in Hollywood. Some people only feel comfortable in a small town in Montana while others find heaven in Manhattan. For some people, the three most important career considerations are the same as what real estate agents say about a house: location, location, and location.

One client, a systems analyst, didn't have location on his goals, wants, and wishes list, but he did list (a) losing 15 pounds and getting in good shape, (b) taking some management courses, (c) spending less time with people he cared little about and more time with those he loved, and (d) becoming a manager in a computer-oriented department or company.

Once listed, a person's goals, wants, and wishes items can then be evaluated for probability, intensity of desire, and time-span considerations. Once completed, the list becomes an easy-to-use component of the gyroscope, a tool for finding one's way through a complex, changing world.

Marketable Skills

To deal with change in a practical rather than fanciful way, a person must also assess marketable skills. This again takes the form of a list. It includes abilities, talents, aptitudes, skills, personality facets, and attitudes that an employer may find valuable. Don't include skills that haven't been proven by demonstration, experience, or education. However, do include skills that can be reoriented, perfected, or used in a different way. For instance, a high school math teacher would naturally list skills like designing lesson plans and teaching classes. Stated that way, the skills would keep the teacher in teaching. But if the teacher wants a job in business, the skill list should translate into an ability to explain complicated concepts and manage groups of people with disparate backgrounds and differing levels of competence.

There are a number of ways to accumulate items for a marketable skills list. One way is to brainstorm all previous jobs, both paid and nonpaid, and jot down all the things done in those jobs, however seemingly insignificant. Fifty to a hundred ideas might emerge. Then take the long list, simplify and organize it.

Among other techniques for exploring skills are *card sorts*. Their hands-on, gamelike quality is often a welcome change from paper-and-pencil exercises, tests, or long interviews. A pair of these products currently popular with career counselors, *Motivated Skills Card Sort*[22] and *SkillScan*,[23] each consists of a deck of cards with different skills described on separate cards. Both produce a matrix that groups skills according to how well a client thinks he or she can perform them and how much the client would like to do so. The technique can help compile a list of employable skills and provide good data for a résumé. Just as the codified list of wants and wishes produces one dimension for our personal guidance system, a marketable skills list, kept fresh and up-to-date, provides the second dimension.

Personal Yardstick

The third dimension makes our personal guidance system complete. It is the beginning of our individual yardstick. Building it requires a list of descriptive words as diverse as apples, trucks, dogs, and charity. It specifies the various qualities that bring enjoyment to work and life. Strong personality characteristics that need accommodating, environments in which to flourish, skills that a client takes delight in using, the types of people one wants to work with, money to pay for the lifestyle one desires, situations that are most stimulating and gratifying—any can be the ingredients that combine to produce career and life enthusiasm.

A tightened version of this descriptive word list becomes a client's personal yardstick. The ultimate items might include such things as having financial security, feeling like an expert, using analytical skills to improve results, being a member of the team that makes important decisions, affiliating with respected organizations, having opportunities to meet and develop a relationship with a potential marriage partner, and helping others be more successful. Just as with the other two lists, the yardstick should be based on careful assessment techniques like tests, self-exploratory exercises, and personal histories.

These three components of the personal gyroscope—goals, wants, and wishes; marketable skills; and the personal yardstick—are simplified into three succinct pages, each likely containing less than ten items. While a client can look back on the longer original lists, the gyroscope itself is a compact document. Since it is easy to consult, clients can turn to it several times each year, with or without professional counsel, to make sure they're on target or make course corrections if not.

Putting Clients on Course

Now let's return to the three clients we originally discussed—Phil Stockton, the Denver telecommunications manager; Margo Crystal, the 23-year-old college graduate; and Bill Kaible, the corporate lawyer. Each faced different challenges. While their solutions varied, the *techniques* used to approach the challenges were similar. Each constructed a simplified personal gyroscope for career-life planning and used it to evaluate and guide their changes.

▶   Phil Stockton, the Denver man considering a move to Atlanta, found discussing his goals, wants, and wishes list particularly meaningful. It stimulated thoughtful discussions about how much he loved his friends and family life, the home they were so carefully remodeling bit by bit, the joy and comfort of watching his children interact with their grandparents, and being in the area he had called home for his entire life. That sense of security and roots was as important to Stockton as adventure is to the jet pilot, influence to the politician, or nurturing to the nursery school teacher.

Stockton's career and personal assessments motivated him to decline the Atlanta job. But he started a thorough, although part-time, job search in the Denver area, while remaining on his old job. Within six months, he had two offers that had great appeal to him. One required travel and long office hours. The other, with a data and voice systems company, didn't pay as much but offered security without the travel and extended work hours. Since home time and a stable environment were essential to Phil Stockton, his choice could not have been more clear.

▶ Margo Crystal, the eager young woman with nowhere to go, seemed to find a new puzzle piece for her career-life picture with each assessment technique she encountered. The results of her tests painted the picture of a very ambitious, responsibility-seeking young woman, willing to take risks. The tests confirmed that she was extremely outgoing, action-oriented, and practical, that she preferred to be the leader in most situations, and that she enjoyed math, writing, analysis, and logic. She was highly responsible and could be tough-minded when the situation called for it.

Crystal was more ambitious than 95 percent of the adult female population. Her social presence was higher than 75 percent of adults. And she was more interested than 90 percent of either men or women in business management. She tested higher than 80 percent of females in merchandising and had interests that were very similar to people already employed as marketing executives, investment managers, and elected public officials.

Of course, these were only a small portion of her self-assessment results. But when combined with her background experiences, skills, and ambitions, graduate business school began to loom large on her horizon. Practically speaking, however, Crystal needed both to acquire some money and quality business experience before applying to a business school several years down the road.

When she whittled down the list of characteristics that reflected her personal satisfaction in making vocational and personal choices, she found that her personal yardstick consisted of seven items. These would guide her questions in interviews and job investigations, help her correct her course when she was feeling dissatisfied, and give her direction in planning her pursuits.

Crystal's personal yardstick listed: (a) be a professional specialist (rather than a generalist) who is considered an expert and whose advice is taken seriously; (b) analyze ideas and information and have others give real consideration to them; (c) work with highly motivated people in a fast-paced environment; (d) advise, consult, manage, and lead; (e) make enough money to be completely independent and to enjoy some travel and a comfortable lifestyle; (f) keep learning and feeling challenged; and (g) make time for friends and dates so there's a chance to meet a potential husband.

After extensively investigating local clothing, fashion, and merchandising businesses, Crystal secured an entry-level marketing position in a large clothing manufacturing firm. The pay was lower than she had counted on, but within eight months she was twice promoted and given healthy raises. She found an apartment with two other young women and engaged in a very active social life.

▶ On Kaible's marketable skills list were items like negotiate, mediate, persuade, observe, evaluate, analyze, synthesize information, and make others feel at ease both in normal and tense situations. Not only did he weave these and other skills into his resume, but he developed short vignettes to illustrate his proficiency in using them.

While Kaible confirmed his desire to end his formal law career, he decided that his legal background could help him in business management where, it turned out, he more naturally belonged. He investigated human resource management positions in midsized to large corporations, where he could use his legal knowledge regarding employee rights and benefits as well as his skills related to negotiating labor contracts. At the same time, he could integrate these legal skills into the management side of business and progress, he hoped, toward top management.

After several months of searching, Kaible accepted the position of assistant director of human resources for a large company providing ground and air delivery service throughout the United States. Exposed to an entirely new set of co-workers, Kaible developed many new friendships. As he put his divorce behind him, he began dating. In both his work and personal life, Bill Kaible set a new course.

Attitudes

A gyroscope doesn't just function. It must be powered. And what gives energy to a career and life planning gyroscope is attitude. As psychologist Albert Bandura notes, in order for people to cope with new career paths, they need a resilient belief in themselves (which he calls *self-efficacy*), especially concerning the things they are trying to learn and do. "The research suggests that in order for people to be able to take on challenges and to persevere in the face of difficulties," says Bandura, "they really have to have an *optimistic* sense of their self-efficacy. If you have a realistic sense of self-efficacy, you will only believe you can do what you have done."[24] The realities of life are failures, adversities, setbacks, and inequities; realists simply succumb to these.

Dr. Bandura's research demonstrates a direct relationship between people's attitudes about acquiring skills and the way they deal with taxing situations. "Those who believe that ability is sort of an inherent, innate, or inherently fixed attribute are the ones that are very threatened by failure, because that indicates they're dumb," he explains. "Whereas with those who really look upon complex decision making as an acquirable skill, errors don't have any negative value. They can learn how to master a particular activity from their mistakes. Given a choice of doing something in which they look good, or something where they can expand their knowledge and competencies, they prefer expanding their competencies."

Attitudes, then, have a profound impact on the effectiveness of a personal gyroscope. And attitudes also influence the balance between work and professional life. When we work too long and hard, we need time to relax or play. When we relax or play too long we can experience boredom, if not fall into a state of ennui.

Attitudes heavily help guide our gyroscope. Maintenance keeps it in good working condition. It should be checked frequently to assure its parts are correctly adjusted. This means reviewing and updating its three bases of information at least once or twice a year. Our gyroscope then stands ready to assist in evaluating impending changes, to help one manage obstacles, and to direct a future course.

As Richard Bolles says about the career and life planning process, "What tools I'm trying to teach you are tools for a lifetime. You probably won't have to use all of them all at once as you're doing now, but you'll surely be using some of them almost every month for the rest of your life. Things have to keep changing."[25]

Things *will* keep changing, without fail. How well we will respond to such passages is often determined before we even arrive. The key is in the planning.

Notes

1   *Random House Dictionary of the English Language, The Unabridged Edition* (1967), 633.

2   Interview with John Krumboltz, October 19, 1989.

3   Interview with Lili Pratt, October 5, 1989.

4   Interview with Patricia A. Templin, September 15, 1989.

5   Interview with Edward Chiosso, September 6, 1989.

6   Interview with Richard Bolles, September 20, 1989.

7   Interview with David Krantz, September 6, 1989.

8   Thomas J. Peters and Robert H. Waterman, Jr., *In Search of Excellence, Lessons from America's Best-Run Companies* (New York: Harper & Row, 1982), 119–155.

9   Interview with Sally Brew, September 13, 1989.

10 Richard N. Bolles, *The Quick Job-Hunting Map* (Berkeley: Ten Speed Press, 1979).

11 Arthur F. Miller and Ralph T. Mattson, *The Truth About You* (Berkeley: Ten Speed Press, 1989).

12 Interview with Harrison Gough, September 26, 1989.

13 Carol Gilligan, Ravenna Helson, James Picano, and Penelope Kegel-Folm are a few such scholars.

14 Karl E. Weick, *The Social Psychology of Organizing,* 2nd ed. (New York: Addison-Wesley, 1979), 194–201.

15 Isabel Briggs Myers, *Myers-Briggs Type Indicator®* (Palo Alto, CA: Consulting Psychologists Press, 1977).

16 E. K. Strong, Jr., Jo-Ida Hansen, and David P. Campbell, *Strong Interest Inventory* (Palo Alto, CA: Consulting Psychologists Press, 1985).

17 Interview with Al Hammer, September 26, 1989.

18 While there are other aptitude testing firms, Johnson O'Connor is an example of quality.

19 Will Schutz, *FIRO-B* (Palo Alto, CA: Consulting Psychologists Press, 1967).

20 Harrison G. Gough, *California Psychological Inventory* (Palo Alto, CA: Consulting Psychologists Press, 1987).

21 Joint Committee on Testing Practices, *Code of Fair Testing Practices in Education* (Washington, DC, 1988).

22 *Motivated Skills Card Sort* (San Jose, CA: Career Research & Testing, 1981).

23 Lesah Beckhusen and Lorraine Gazzano, *SkillsScan*ᴹ (Orinda, CA: Author, 1987).

24 Interview with Albert Bandura, September 23, 1989.

25 Interview with Richard Bolles, September 20, 1989.

Some of the people and companies mentioned as examples have been disguised to protect their identity.

Bibliography

Publications

Bandura, A. (1986). *Social foundations of thought and action: A social cognitive theory.* Englewood Cliffs, NJ: Prentice-Hall.

Beckhusen, L., & Gazzano, L. (1987). *SkillScan™ professional pack.* Orinda, CA: Beckhusen & Gazzano.

Bolles, R. N. (1985). *The quick job-hunting map.* Berkeley, CA: Ten Speed Press.

Motivated Skills Card Sort. (1981). San Jose, CA: Career Research & Testing.

Davidson, S. L. (1989). Career counseling with adults: A metaphor for change. *Career Planning and Adult Development Journal.* San Jose, CA: Career Planning and Adult Development Network.

Gardner, H. (1983). *Frames of mind: The theory of multiple intelligences.* New York: Basic Books.

Gardner, J. W. (1964). *Self renewal: The individual and the innovative society.* New York: Harper & Row.

Gilligan, C. (1982). *In a different voice: Psychological theory and women's development.* Cambridge, MA: Harvard University Press.

Gough, H. G. (1987). *California Psychological Inventory administrator's guide.* Palo Alto, CA: Consulting Psychologists Press.

Gould, R. L. (1987). *Transformations: Growth and change in adult life.* New York: Simon & Schuster.

Haldane, B. (1988). *Career satisfaction and success: How to know and manage your strengths.* New York: AMACOM.

Hansen, J. C., & Campbell, D. P. (1985). *The Strong manual.* Palo Alto, CA: Consulting Psychologists Press.

Hansen, J. C. (1984). *The Strong user's guide.* Palo Alto, CA: Consulting Psychologists Press.

Helson, R., & Wink, P. (1987). Two conceptions of maturity examined in the findings of a longitudinal study. *Journal of Personality and Social Psychology, 53,* 531–541.

Helson, R., Mitchell, V., & Moane, G. (1984). Personality and patterns of adherence and nonadherence to the social clock. *Journal of Personality of Social Psychology, 46* (5), 1079–1096.

Holland, J. L. (1973). *Making vocational choices.* Englewood Cliffs, NJ: Prentice-Hall.

Joint Committee on Testing Practices. (1988). *Code of fair testing practices in education.* Washington, DC.

Jung, C. G. (1971). *Psychological types.* Princeton, NJ: Princeton University Press.

Kaye, B. L. (1982). *Up is not the only way.* Englewood Cliffs, NJ: Prentice-Hall.

Kegel-Flom, P. (1988). Women optometry students: How qualified? *American Journal of Optometry and Physiological Optics, 65* (8), 666–673.

Kegel-Flom, P. (1983). *Personality traits in effective clinical teachers.* Unpublished manuscript. Houston, TX: University of Houston.

Krumboltz, J. (in press). *Career Beliefs Inventory.* Palo Alto, CA: Consulting Psychologists Press.

Leibowitz, Z. B., Farren, C., & Kaye, B. L. (1986). *Designing career development systems.* San Francisco: Jossey-Bass.

Levinson, D. J., Darrow, C. N., Klein, E. B., Levinson, M. H., & McKee, B. (1978). *The seasons of a man's life.* New York: Knopf.

McAllister, L. W. (1988). *A practical guide to CPI interpretation* (2nd ed.). Palo Alto, CA: Consulting Psychologists Press.

Megargee, E. I. (1972). *The California Psychological Inventory handbook.* San Francisco: Jossey-Bass.

Miller, A. F., & Mattson, R. T. (1989). *The truth about you.* Berkeley, CA: Ten Speed Press.

Myers, I. B., & McCaulley, M. H. (1985). *Manual: A guide to the development and use of the Myers-Briggs Type Indicator.* Palo Alto, CA: Consulting Psychologists Press.

Osipow, S. H. (1983). *Theories of career development* (3rd ed.). Englewood Cliffs, NJ: Prentice-Hall.

Papp, P. (1983). *The process of change.* New York: Guilford Press.

Peters, T. J., & Waterman, R. H., Jr. (1982). *In search of excellence: Lessons from America's best-run companies.* New York: Harper & Row.

Picano, J. J. (1989). Development and validation of a life history index of adult adjustment for women. *Journal of Personality Assessment, 53*(2), 308–318.

Riverin-Simard, D. (1990, Dec.). Adult vocational trajectory. *Career Development Journal, 39,* 129–142.

Riverin-Simard, D. (1988). *Phases of working life.* Montreal: Meridian Press.

Schutz, W. (1967). *The FIRO Awareness Scales.* Palo Alto, CA: Consulting Psychologists Press.

Schutz, W. (1978). *The FIRO Awareness Scales manual.* Palo Alto, CA: Consulting Psychologists Press.

Sternberg, R. J. (1988). *The triarchic mind: A new theory of human intelligence.* New York: Penguin Books.

Vaillant, G. E. (1977). *Adaptation to life.* Boston: Little, Brown.

Waterman, J. A. (1987) *A client's guide to the FIRO-B.* Palo Alto: CA: Consulting Psychologists Press.

Weick, K. E. (1979). *The social psychology of organizing* (2nd ed). Reading, MA: Addison-Wesley.

Whitbourne, S., & Weinstock, C. (1979). Adulthood: To be and to become. *Contemporary Psychology, 24*(11).

Interviews

Avis, Joan P., Professor, Department of Counseling and Educational Psychology, University of San Francisco. Interview on September 12, 1989.

Bandura, Albert, David Starr Jordan Professor of Social Science and Psychology, Stanford University. Interview on September 23, 1989.

Bolles, Richard N., Author of *What Color Is Your Parachute?* Interview on September 20, 1989.

Brew, Sally, Lockheed Missile and Space Company, Organizational Development Specialist. Interview on September 13, 1989.

Chiosso, Ed, Coordinator, Guidance and Counseling, San Mateo County Office of Education. Interview on September 6, 1989.

Gough, Harrison G., Professor Emeritus, University of California, Berkeley, California. Interview on September 26, 1989.

Guterman, Mark, President, G & G Associates, Career and Organizational Counseling Firm. Interview on October 31, 1989.

Hammer, Al, Senior Product Developer, Consulting Psychologists Press, Palo Alto, California. Interview on September 26, 1989.

Krantz, David O., Senior Vice President, Consulting Psychologists Press, Palo Alto, California. Interview on September 6, 1989.

Krumboltz, John, Professor of Education and Psychology, Stanford University. Interview on October 19, 1989.

Markoff, Annabelle, Director, Learning Disabilities Clinic, San Mateo, California. Interview on September 6, 1989.

Pratt, Lili, partner in M^2, San Francisco, California and Career Strategist at Stanford Business School, Career Development Office. Interview on October 5, 1989.

Ransom, David, Director of San Francisco office of Johnson-O'Connor Research Foundation, Inc. Interview on September 14, 1989.

Templin, Patricia A., Senior Vice President, Right Associates, Cupertino, California. Interview on September 15, 1989.

Three Suggested Exercises

General Note to the Career Counselor: While the following exercises are extensive enough to be used as the basis for an entire course in career and life planning, they can be modified or simplified to meet various time limits—even a brief discussion. They are intended for either individual or group work. In addition to these exercises, any comprehensive career and life planning class or counseling sessions should include investigation of various kinds of jobs, realities of the workplace, information about the job hunt, the résumé, and interview coaching. Quite simply, what you are striving for in these exercises is to help clients clearly articulate the characteristics by which they chart their courses, use their talents, and make their choices—in other words, a carefully constructed but easily updated personal gyroscope.

Exercises follow.

Counselor Note Concerning the First Exercise: The purpose of the first exercise is to sensitize clients to the changes affecting their lives. It can take the form of a group exercise or an individual essay, or it can even be adapted to an audio or video report.

Exercise 1: Personal Change

1. Draw a long horizontal line to represent your life. Designate below the line periodic ages (10, 20, and 30, for instance). Extend the line to age 80 or so to portray your probable life span. Put a vertical line through the horizontal life line at the point of your present age. On your life line put a dot where you experienced big changes, that is, changes that you remember as significant, whether or not others would consider them so. Designate each dot with one or more of the following abbreviations, according to the definitions shown:

    A = avocational change   **C** = child influenced change
    D = individual development   **$** = financial change
    E = change imposed by   **I** = internally promoted change
         external events, pressures,   **R** = relationship change
         or people   **W** = work/nonwork change
    G = geographic change   **S** = school change
    M = miscellaneous other changes

2. Mark the extended part of your line with anticipated and desired future changes. (See one woman's life line changes in the accompanying example.)

3. Divide your group into pairs or triads if this is a group exercise.

4. First, discuss all or a selection of your changes and the way they affected your life and the lives of others. These words may guide your thoughts: inspiring, traumatic, tangible gain or loss, effect on another part of life, dreams shattered or created, common pitfalls, lessons learned, attitude, style of dealing with, planning and information, quickness of response, patterns, and guidance.

5. Now discuss the future changes in similar light.

6. Draw conclusions about what you can learn from this exercise.

Example for Exercise 1

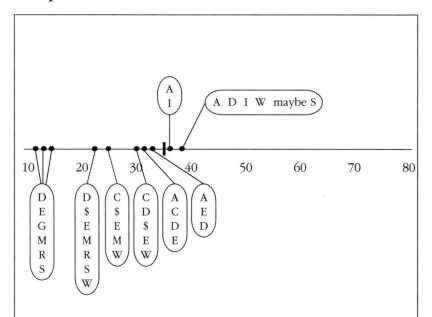

Past: *Realize now that many of my life changes were the
        result of family moves or external happenings.
        I respond well to change—make the most of it and
        experience real personal development. But, without
        external pressures, I don't <u>initiate</u> the changes that
        feel like growth to me.*

Future: *I'm not sure what I'm going to do yet, but I'm sure
        <u>I'm</u> going to initiate it. I need to focus my scattered
        energies on what really motivates me—and <u>get going.</u>
        As I indicated on my chart, I'm going to give myself
        a little time for self-assessment and investigation,
        but I <u>will</u> make some changes!*

Counselor Note Concerning the Second Exercise: This exercise can help clients construct their own personal gyroscopes. Optimum results are usually gained when you help the client gather a large amount of personal information first (through tests, analysis of previous experiences, self-assessment exercises, discussions, and personal insight), then cull and simplify it.

Exercise 2: Creating a Personal Gyroscope

1. Explore the following aspects of your personal-career life:

   Your skills
   Your patterns of motivation
   What comes most naturally to you
   Your self-concept and image
   Your wants, wishes, desires, ambitions, hopes, dreams, ideas,
       and plans
   A list of career opportunities that interest you
   Personal attitudes concerning your potential and options
   Personal assets and limitations.

2. What people count most and/or are most influential in your life? What effect might your plans have on them? *From their point of view,* what is important—for them and for you? Will your actions affect or threaten anyone in particular? What can or do you want to do about that?

3. Next go back over these question once more, but this time in the light of what *others* might say if asked these same questions *about you.*

4. Now you need to decide which pieces of information are important enough to be included in your career-life plan. Whittle down and organize your extensive self-knowledge into three separate synthesized pages: (a) a goals, wants, and wishes list, (b) a marketable skills list, and (c) a personal yardstick.

5. On additional pages, comment on the maintenance of your plan. Include your attitudes, the balance within and between the various facets of your life, and a maintenance log—notes and actions you can take to influence the items on each list.

6. Write or discuss what you learned or can learn from creating such a career-life plan or personal gyroscope.

Counselor Note Concerning the Third Exercise: Now your clients are ready to put their personal gyroscopes to use. They can examine a change in their lives by first considering possible alternatives they might take. Then they can compare how well each alternative fits with the items on their personal gyroscope lists.

You may find that describing the process to clients is cumbersome. Perhaps the example on the next page will help. It shows one possible way to compare alternatives with the items on any of the lists. This particular example demonstrates how one man evaluated two job possibilities using his personal yardstick list. Remember that the way a client defines and rates the items on his or her list will be subjective. No one except that individual can judge how well the items fit with the alternatives. However, when he or she compares the items, the necessity for additional information often becomes apparent.

The point to get across to your clients is this: Use the lists of the personal gyroscope to determine how appropriate possible alternatives are. If a client uses his or her personal gyroscope but says the resulting conclusions do not "feel right," you can be sure the gyroscope has not been calibrated carefully enough. If this happens, help your client do some additional self-assessment to fine tune his or her gyroscope—to make sure the right items are on each list. Then try using it again.

Exercise 3: Using the Gyroscope to Cope With Life Changes

1. Select at least one change you have either experienced in the past, are facing now, or anticipate encountering. Consider various choices you might make in responding to that change and list them as alternatives a, b, etc.

2. Next, compare each of those alternatives to the lists of your personal gyroscope. How well does each alternative fit with your lists? It's true that we seldom find the perfect choice. But your gyroscope can help you identify what important pieces of information you may be missing and which alternatives are better than others. It can also pinpoint components of a choice that will be inadequately fulfilled for you.

In the accompanying example, we see that "sales rep in a music instrument distribution company" seems a better choice than "owning and managing own music store." However, one of the items on the personal yardstick list, "Be a central part of my community," was not particularly a good fit with the sales rep job. This reminds the man that he will need to find avenues in his personal life, or creatively invent ways through his work, to progress toward making a prominent place for himself in his community.

Don't forget to use all the lists of your personal gyroscope, and remember to maintain it. Keep track of your attitudes concerning its maintenance, and give it regular check-ups. Keeping it up to date means it is there for your use whenever you need it.

Example for Exercise 3

Key: 2 = Very Good Fit   1 = Fairly Good Fit   0 = Neutral   −1 = Poor Fit   −2 = Very Poor Fit

Priorities	Weight (10 pts tops)	Alternative A Sales Rep. in Music Dist. Co.		Alternative B Own & Manage Music Store	
1. Interface personally with people to give them quality service	10 x	2 =	20	2 =	20
2. Time flexibility and independence	10 x	2 =	20	−2 =	−20
3. Be a central part of my community	9 x	−1 =	−9	2 =	18
4. Use music knowledge background	8 x	1 =	8	1 =	8
5. Enough money for present lifestyle	8 x	2 =	16	−1* =	−8
6. Have significant responsibility with authority to execute it	7 x	2 =	14	2 =	14
7. Less congested geographic area	6 x	2 =	12	2 =	12
8. Move around—not at a desk all day	5 x	2 =	10	2 =	10
Totals:			91		54

* for some time

2

• • • • • • • • •

Career Development for Empowerment in a Changing Work World

DENNIS T. JAFFE AND CYNTHIA D. SCOTT

Introduction

The nature of the organization, what the organization needs from employees, and what employees want and need from the organization are all evolving. The organization is changing and needs different skills, attitudes, and behavior from employees. This has changed the career ladder and expectations of how one can grow in the organization. The skills needed today are moving away from those of narrowly specialized technicians and toward those of generalists who have a broad overview of the organization and are able to change roles and apply many skills in their work. Companies are also asking for more accountability and offering less security and stability. Employees are seeking work that offers more meaning, more variety, more creativity, and greater opportunities to contribute and take initiative. These changes are shaking the fabric of the organization, and as a result, career development is taking on greater importance. While companies can no longer offer steady, predictable career paths and job security, they still do not want their most effective and competent employees to move on to other companies. Career development increasingly becomes a competitive tool for retaining employees and helping them develop the new competencies and attitudes needed for the new organization.

This chapter is divided into two parts. Part 1 looks at a new concept in career development arising from the needs of a changing workplace. It uses the example of an innovative high tech company that implemented a program using career development as a tool for empowerment in response to the employees' perceived lack of advancement opportunities and management's need to retain its valuable talent. Part 2 is a condensed version of the workbook that was designed and successfully used as part of a companywide program in career development.

Part 1: A New Concept in Career Development

The Changing Workplace

The workplace is changing at an incredible rate. The sum of these changes requires a major change in the way organizations are designed—not just a change of size, rules, or procedures, but a shift in the way that work is organized and companies are structured. The traditional pyramidal organization is dying. A host of pressures, such as downsizing, mergers, restructuring, productivity and quality demands, and global competition, is changing the nature of the organization. The pyramid is being replaced by a much flatter, more flexible organization that continually adapts, innovates, and changes. Major changes are taking place in organizations, which have significant implications for career development.

The New Network Organization. To a greater or lesser degree, every organization is shifting away from the traditional organization to a new form where communication is more important, where temporary project groups form and dissolve, where people do many tasks, where collaboration and teamwork are essential, and where continual improvement of quality and effectiveness are expected. Some organizations are moving in this direction faster than others, but even the most traditional companies are adopting network structures to innovate and adapt.

The new workplace is less concerned with status and role and more focused on personal authority, communication skills, collaborative ability, and ability to perform many tasks. The scope of authority and responsibility grows in the new organization as every person, not just top executives, are concerned with the overall strategy and improvement of the organization. If an individual cannot look at broader issues, help the organization as a whole, and take on many tasks, he or she will not succeed. The skills for effectiveness in the new network organization are not the skills that made one effective in the stable hierarchy. People trained in the old ways need to get themselves retrained, or they risk becoming obsolete.

The New Work Contract. The organization expects different things from its employees and offers different incentives. The expectation of job security and lifetime employment is no longer tenable, so people must keep themselves useful and relevant to the company. People want more meaning, involvement, information, and creativity from their work. They are motivated less by money, status, promotions, and security. Pay and evaluation are based more on performance and results, rather than on simply getting one's job done. These new expectations are somewhat upsetting to people who have bought into the traditional work contract or who still operate under old assumptions. Old-line employees are very upset and angry at what they perceive as a change in the rules in the middle of the game, but they need to adapt and learn the new ways.

Empowerment and Learning Are the New Game. Workplaces need employees to take more responsibility and to be more innovative and creative in what they do. This is true even at the lowest levels of the organization. People need to take more responsibility and to be part of figuring out the best way to get the job done. "The old ways won't work," as one progressive company states it, becomes the new operational reality. People need to take initiative and look to themselves to find their own path of career development. The old way of hooking oneself to a boss or mentor and pleasing only that person no longer works in quite the same way. People must learn new skills and shift the ways they work.

Multicompetency and Collaboration Are Power. The new workplace and the new, fast-growing organization need people who know how to do several jobs, not just one narrow one. People who have several skills that they can blend or use alternately are more important and powerful than those with one skill. In order to succeed in the organization, employees are making themselves more marketable by learning how to do other people's jobs. In addition, they are finding that the skills of working with people, doing projects together, getting information, raising tough issues, and creating synergy in a team are becoming as important as technical competence. In the new workplace, technical skills are still used, but used in teams with other people.

Self-awareness and Self-management Need Development. Career planning needs to begin with an inner-directed plan that includes personal values, interests, and goals as well as clear direction for development of not just one, but several, competencies. People need to generate their own career plan, or they risk feeling burned out and adrift in the workplace. Since the workplace shifts so continually, people need to create a strong inner sense of direction and identity. They cannot expect their manager, or their workplace, to offer them either.

Career Development for Empowerment

How do employees who are caught up in these changes feel? The *psychological contract,* or set of expectations between an individual and the organization, has shifted. People no longer can expect their organization to take care of them, like a good parent, in return for loyalty. Nor can they expect regular promotions or advancement in a flat organization. As the organization becomes leaner and flatter, the traditional opportunities to move up are severely limited. In fact, the whole concept of career development seems to be changing in the new organization.

What does an employee do to adapt to the new organizational realities? The major change the individual has to make is to become portable—that is, to develop a broad-based set of skills and competencies that are relevant to many organizations. The employee cannot move up a single organizational ladder, but must continually learn new skills and move in new, often unexpected, directions. Since technical skills are changing so quickly, as are the organization's needs, the key skill is not in any single content area, but the skill of *learning how to learn.*

The traditional concept of career development as a set of personal goals and strategic moves toward greater achievement and advancement along a clearly defined career path must be replaced with a broader, more diverse, more flexible plan. In the new organizational environment, personal career development becomes a daily issue. The individual needs to think strategically and develop a personal learning plan for ongoing development.

Organizations acknowledge that they must provide more intensive and regular support for employees' career development in the workplace in order to temper the confusion, bitterness, and difficulty that employees may feel in response to changes in what they can expect from the organization. Career development is also a tool that can help retain and attract people to the company.

If the organization is continually changing, then it must provide change management resources for its individual employees. In fact, organizations that provide such services to employees are finding that they are a new source of competitive advantage. In organizations where people are already adequately paid, what additional motivating incentives can be offered to recruit, retain and encourage employees? The answers are that companies can provide employees with opportunities to learn as well as more meaningful jobs, more opportunities to participate in the governance of the organization, and the chance to take on different tasks and pursue different interests.

This new enhanced role is far different than the traditional concept of the employee. It is a role that we have begun to call *organizational citizenship,* in that it looks more like the rights and responsibilities of a citizen of a community than of a corporate employee. The difficulty facing many organizations is how to teach and support their employees to take on this new role. It doesn't come easily. At the start, it demands that the individual take more responsibility for charting a career and future path and for finding ways to contribute to the organization.

The goal of career development is to help the employee focus on his or her future in the organization and to help the employee pursue a career path that involves continual learning. The concept of *empowerment* is one of an expanded sense of accountability, self-responsibility, and more control over one's role in the organization. No longer is the work role determined only by the employer and supervisor. In the new workplace, the work role, like everything else, is negotiated, with the employee having input and making suggestions.

One large high tech company became committed to this concept. The CEO decided that career development was a corporate priority. There was a selfish need for this: Other companies were raiding the talent from his company, and he needed to retain employees as the company grew from its start-up phase into professional management. The need for succession planning, that is, for helping managers develop people to meet the organization's long-term staffing needs, had just emerged. Also, there was a perception that promotions were based more on politics than merit and so people saw career development as moving into other companies rather than evolving from within.

The solution was to design a systemwide career development program. The core concept was to enhance the role of the manager or supervisor to include not just performance appraisal but also some shared responsibility for helping each employee with career development. The shift had to take place on three levels in the organization:

▶ *Individual mind-sets:* People had to learn new ways of thinking about careers and seeing their own career.

▶ *Work relationships:* Supervisors and employees had to include exploring new work options, new skill development, and continual learning and growth as part of their appraisal system. It needed to be a shared responsibility.

▶ *Organizational structures and norms:* The organization needed to value career development and support its use by mandating career planning and offering resources. It also had to design, support, and reward development, retraining, and job redefinitions as part of its policy.

The company instituted a total career development effort, which was to be a joint responsibility of the supervisor and employee. Every year, in addition to the performance review, the supervisor would be responsible for holding a career development discussion with the employee. The employee would be responsible for scheduling the discussion and preparing for it by completing the exercises in a workbook, a condensed version of which constitutes Part 2 of this chapter. A workshop was also designed for supervisors that taught them the basic skills of career coaching, and the program was kicked off with an orientation for the whole company.

The initial result was that career development became part of the everyday considerations about job and performance. Employees could inquire into future possibilities and make plans for new assignments. Supervisors began to see themselves in a new role as guides for career development and learning. Everyone began to talk about how they could encourage personal development. Employees looked for opportunities inside the company before they looked to other companies. The program became an attractive recruiting tool for new employees. People in departments began to look at learning opportunities they could offer and to find ways to make use of internal personnel, even if it took some retraining. One important discovery was that it was just as effective to offer someone inside the company the opportunity to learn a new job as to try to hire from outside. Attention was focused on the people who were there.

The career development program became the one essential component of the shift in this workplace to the new network form of organization. It was also an important marker in the maturing of the company from a high-tech start-up that had no thought of internal development and the future to a company that was concerned with long-term survival. In the new workplace, every employee takes personal responsibility for his or her own learning and finds that, while the organization cannot offer security, it can offer support for learning, growth, and development.

The next section of this chapter presents an example of the material one might find in a career development workbook prepared for employees of an organization offering career development as part of its incentive program. It is designed to be a self-study guide for a person to use on his or her own. The resulting self-study can be used as part of a career development exploration, with a counselor helping the individual to explore, develop, and interpret the exercises. It can also be used by a work team, or an individual and his or her manager, as part of a supervisory/career development process. We suggest that the workbook be used as part of the general employee development and supervision process within an organization. It is a tool for developing internal commitment to a changing and difficult workplace, and for individuals to begin to see that their perceptions of their future, and the steps they take to reach it, can be part of their everyday work process. It is a management tool that develops each individual in a work team, as well as an individual growth tool that helps the individual chart a course.*

Part 2: A Guide to Employee Career Development

Only you create your career. You are the only one who can decide what you want and where you want to go. You must choose to proceed upon the difficult path of self-development, and you need to take the initiative. When you make your choices, many resources are available to you. Your company offers resources, people, programs, and tools. This guide is organized to support your career planning process. Although you are the person primarily responsible for your career, you draw upon other resources and people to help you. This guide makes you aware of the possibilities and helps you organize your planning. You may want to review your career goals, plans, and progress with your manager, a mentor, or a support person in your workplace or personal life.

Some Initial Questions

Where You Are You Going? The job you are in now will not last forever. It will evolve and change. Even if it could, you probably wouldn't want it to remain static. Most likely you see yourself doing something different— growing, developing new skills and interests, seeking new challenges—in the future. Some people have a clear vision of where they are going and a plan to get there. Others want something more, or something different from their work, but they are less clear about how to get there.

Exploring, planning, and creating your future at work is called *career development*. This is a guide for your own process of career planning. Career development will help you:

▶ Understand the resources and activities for career development that exist at your company

▶ Identify where you are now in your career development

▶ Explore where you want to go in the future

▶ Discover new possibilities and options

▶ Develop and implement your career plan

---

* For further information about this program and other resources used in such programs, you can contact the HeartWork Group in San Francisco. Please note that the workbook and the program is copyrighted and cannot be used without permission of the publisher.

What Is Career Development? *Career development* is your continual search and striving for the achievement of your own potential and fulfillment in your work and your expression of this in your work today. It involves understanding yourself in terms of your potential, your fullest possible capabilities, your personal values, your interests, and your environment. It also involves seeking opportunities, making discoveries, taking risks, growing, and taking action. Career development is working today with one eye on your future. It is knowing where you are going. It is not a plan or a blueprint fixed in advance. Developing your career is a process, continually unfolding, shifting, and changing.

A career is a sequence of jobs and other experiences (e.g., education, involvements, community service) where each activity is linked in relation to a personal plan or set of goals. A career is a life structure that you create and build. It is unique to you. It represents the way that you develop your specific potentials and get what you want from your lifetime of working. There is a difference between a job and a career. A job is the specific position you have right now. Some people spend their lives moving from job to job, with no connection between them. You get more satisfaction, success, creativity, and involvement from your work if it expresses your personal career plan.

Your career development is in your hands. You can create opportunities and set your direction, or you can drift. You can plan for what you really want, or you can settle for what you get.

Why Do Career Planning? Many people don't give much thought to their career. They learn and master their job and wait for an opportunity to surface in the form of a job opening at a higher level. They believe their career just happens to them—all they need to succeed is to do their job; the rest will follow.

This strategy is unwise for today. The traditional career progression up the organizational ladder just doesn't exist anymore. The company you work for is probably not a traditional company organized in a stable pyramid with each grade or job precisely defined and clearly specified. It is an organization in continual motion—growing, shifting, changing, diversifying, evolving. There are no standard career progressions or orderly process of promotion and development.

But what if you are satisfied with what you are doing? Why worry or think about the future? The reason is that everything is changing.

▶   First, your feelings about your job will change. In the first few years of a job there is excitement as you master its demands. Then it can become stale or even routine. Your own performance may decline as well, and you may even begin to burn out. Will the same job that challenges or satisfies you today still feel that way next year?

▶ Second, your company needs for you to continually increase your skills and talents. Competition is intense. Your company's major competitive edges are the skill and dedication of its people and its responsiveness to change. Taking care of your career development is one way to prepare yourself to master change as it takes place. If you don't stay current professionally, your profession may pass you by!

▶ Third, the opportunities that exist are not always obvious. Everyone is unique and has the capacity to develop new skills and work in new areas. Your career development may lie in finding new worlds to conquer and new types of work that build on your existing skills. You may move into another area or take a job that combines your current skills with new ones. In order to achieve your own fullest potential, you need to search for opportunities, not wait for them to come find you.

▶ Finally, you need to keep checking, because the opportunities that exist are also changing. New opportunities are opening while others close. You need to keep yourself current on what is happening, or you may miss the boat! And as you develop, more options will open to you.

How Much Help Do You Need? People have different needs around career development. Three styles of career searching are defined below. Identify which style fits you to understand how much you need to focus on career development.

▶ *Wanderers* have unclear goals or no clear direction. They need a lot of help to explore themselves and get into greater focus. You are probably a Wanderer if

> You are not sure where you are going in your life
>
> You feel fine taking the job you are offered
>
> You don't think about the future—you focus on today
>
> You aren't sure what you like to do

▶ *Directeds* have goals involving movement within their chosen field of expertise. They seek to expand their skills within a fairly well-defined arena. You are probably a Directed if

> You like what you are doing
>
> You see yourself getting ahead in your specialty area
>
> You avoid taking risks and don't like a lot of change

▶ *Spanners* have goals that include major shifts into positions outside their field, or want to explore some new directions. You are probably a Spanner if

> You have so many interests you don't know which to pursue
>
> You like to face new challenges and learn new things
>
> You get bored easily
>
> You are feeling burned out or not liking your work

Fifty percent of employees are Directeds.

Twenty-five percent are Wanderers, and 25 percent are Spanners.

From the descriptions above, try to decide which type you are. Do you need to work on getting into focus (Wanderer), or are you on the verge of a major transition (Spanner)? If so, this guide will help you focus on or identify your goals. If you are a Directed, then you will probably need less time for career planning.

Is Career Development an Issue for You? Career development is not an issue for everybody all the time. Sometimes you are content to remain on a plateau and other aspects of your life are more important than your career. At a few times in your life, however, your future, your work, and your career take center stage. You may be in a midlife career crisis, or you may be agonizing about a potential direction for a next step, or you may need to make a major shift or look at where you are. For those moments—or crises—taking time to assess where you are in your career can be among the best gifts you can give yourself.

Every life has a series of stages of development. Usually you enter a new life stage after you successfully resolve a developmental crisis. This then leads to a period of stability and clear direction, which then ends with another period of turmoil and transition. Life stages can be predictable, as for example when you marry, have children, or take on a special career challenge. Or they can come as a surprise, as when the company asks you to relocate or lays you off. During these transition crises, not only your environment but you yourself are changing. You need to look at what you want and where you are going to take control over getting where you want to be. You may need more or less time and support for this exploration, depending on where you are in your life. Are you in a stable, quiet life stage or a transitional, tumultuous one? If the answer is the latter, then you should take enough time to fully work with the information and exercises presented. The information will be valuable to you as well if you are in a period of stability and calm because you may enter a period of transition in the near future.

The Five Stages of Career Development

There are five stages of career planning. The process really never ends. As you implement your career plan, keep asking yourself how well it is working. If your answer is just fine, then all you need to do is to keep current with your job and with potential career developments and changes, and you will stay on track. If or when your answer becomes no or you're not sure, then you should move back to an earlier stage. During your career you can expect to cycle through these stages several times.

▶ Stage 1: Assess yourself

▶ Stage 2: Explore possibilities

▶ Stage 3: Create a plan

▶ Stage 4: Take action

▶ Stage 5: Evaluate the outcome

Stage 1: Assess Yourself. In this stage you explore your dreams, goals, interests, skills, values, strengths, and weaknesses. You look back at what you have accomplished, how you are doing right now, and what you want to do in the future. The focus is on who you are now and who you can be. You do the work at this stage. You may be familiar with looking at yourself and comfortable with this process. You may already have done much of it. Or it may seem strange and unfamiliar to ask yourself so many questions. You may never have thought about such things. Take as much or as little time as you need.

The pages that follow contain a series of exercises that ask you to focus on your own career goals, interests, and skills. Responding to the questions will help you begin to think about where you are, what you want, and where you are going. Take a few hours to answer them. Remember, they are for you only. You do not need to show them to anyone. However, it often is helpful to solicit other responses and reactions to your ideas.

You may want to share your responses to the exercises with someone you trust. It is often helpful to talk to another person about your career plans. The other person can give you another perspective on your plans. Some of the other people you might talk with include the following:

▶ Your manager

▶ A co-worker who knows you well

▶ Another member of your work team who might share his or her career plans

▶ Your spouse, a close friend, or other family member

Exercise 1: Exploring Yourself

Think about each of the following. Jot down some notes on your reflections.

What I am interested in:

What I am good at:

My most important values in my work and life:

What I would like to learn:

What I would like to develop:

The kind of work environment that I like best or work best in:

The kind of work I would like to do in the future:

What I don't want to be doing in the future:

Exercise 2: Strengths and Weaknesses

It is important for you to have an accurate picture of yourself in order to develop your goals. Take some time and explore your strengths and weaknesses. You might ask some of the people you trust to help you in your self-assessment. Remember, you can change what you know.

My major strengths:

What I can do to develop my strengths:

My major weaknesses:

What I can do to overcome my weaknesses:

Exercise 3: Skills and Activities Inventory

List the different skills, activities, and tasks that you do on your job now or have done in past jobs. Be specific and try to think of as many as you can. You should be able to list many skills (such as preparing reports, writing software, making presentations, calling on prospective customers, organizing projects, word processing, etc.).

Now, go back over your list, and on a scale of 1 to 5 (1 being very little, and 5 being very much) fill in the three columns at the right describing how much you enjoy that activity, how proficient you are at it, and how important it is to you to develop that skill in your future.

Skill or Activity	Enjoy	Proficiency	Importance

Exercise 4: Vision of Your Future Work

Take a few moments to reflect on your dreams and on your vision of where you would like to be in your career a decade from now. Let yourself relax, and try to spin out a waking dream about what your ideal work of the future would look like. Be as specific as you can. Try to suspend the part of you that tries to be practical or realistic or is critical. You can have any dream you want. Try to think about all the different elements of your dream. You might have two or three dreams to spin out. Let yourself have fun with this activity.

Now, jot down some of the key elements of your dream or vision of your ideal future work:

_____

_____

Exercise 5: New Skills and Activities

Add to your list the skills you would like to have and activities that you would like to do in the future or that you think may be important to your future career development:

Skills, knowledge, and abilities I'd like to use in the future:

Skills, knowledge, and abilities I need or want to develop in the future:

Exercise 6: Goals

Visions can be broad and vague. They are there in your imagination. How exactly will they get into your life? This can happen by taking your vision and letting it drive you. Like a long trip, you need markers along the way to tell you that you are on track. These are your goals, the specific things that you will do and accomplish to move toward your dream.

Every dream and vision can be broken down into specific goals and time frames attached to them. Keeping your dream in focus, write some of the specific work, job, and career goals you have for the next ten, three, and one years. Be concrete and specific. A goal is precise—you can know exactly when you have achieved it. Your goals should encompass many areas of your job. For example, it is not enough to say, I will make this job grade by next year. You need to have goals for what you will do in specific areas to achieve this. Like a blueprint, the more precise your goals, the more clear you will be about how to reach them.

In making up goals, start from the farthest point, the closest to your vision, and work backwards. If you go the other way, you run the risk of adopting goals that are not precisely and clearly related to your dreams.

Ten-year goals:

Three-year goals:

One-year goals:

Exercise 7: Activities

Activities represent the next level of specificity. Thinking about your most immediate (one- and three-year) goals, what are some of the specific activities you need to do, learn, or accomplish to reach each one? List the activities in order, next to the goals in the list above, starting with immediate ones.

Stage 2: Explore Possibilities. You have already looked at yourself and explored what you want and your personal goals. Now you need to look outside and begin to explore opportunities. You need to find out what steps to take at your company and some of the options that exist for you there. Career development must take into account what's out there. You may not know what is possible, or your dreams may need a reality check. There may be many possibilities you simply don't know about. There are many ways that you can gather information about what is out there.

In stage 2 you take time to seek out possibilities. If you are unclear (a Wanderer) or if you need a major change (a Spanner), then looking around and seeking resources may lead to incredible discoveries. Don't stick to what you know; move to seek out new people and gather all the information you can. The goal is to discover some of the many pathways for you to pursue, expand, or redefine your dreams and goals. Perhaps you will discover some new ones on the way. This is a stage of moving out, meeting new people, and seeking out possibilities like a private detective.

This section looks at the activities that you can do to begin to gather information, develop your career, and move toward your goals. It is intended to broaden your view of career development.

It looks at

▶ How you can develop yourself in your job

▶ How you can seek information about other jobs

▶ How you can prepare yourself for new challenges and new work

Your Own Job. This is the first area to explore as you begin looking at ideas for opportunities.

▶ *The first step in career development is to do your job well.* You will not be in a position to get a new job if you haven't done well at what you are doing right now. The best indicator of how you will feel in another job is how you are doing now. Many people look to the future and say, things would be better if only I could.... They feel that their problems would dissolve if they had a change. But in fact, how well you do the job you have now suggests how well you will do the next job.

▶ *Your most important ally in career development is your manager.* If you haven't shown that you can master your job, then you are unlikely to receive support to move to a new one.

▶ *When is the right time to leave a job?* Of course, when you get
an offer you can't refuse. But that is somewhat rare. More often,
you have the choice to move or stay. One indicator is whether
you have reached 80 percent mastery of your job. If your job
has become stale, chances are so has your attitude. If you haven't
really learned your job, then you probably aren't ready for a new
one.

▶ *What can you do while you are waiting for a new opportunity to
open up?* The most reasonable answer is to begin a process of job
enlargement, or *growing in place.* This involves looking for ways
to learn new skills and take on new responsibilities in the job you
have. That will demonstrate to others in the company that you
have initiative and that you are able to meet challenges.

▶ *Link what you are doing now with new opportunities.* Opportunities
are not always things that already exist "out there." They are
sometimes possibilities that do not exist until you ask to do them
or make them happen.

▶ *Become a good corporate citizen.* Career development involves
more than improving your job or your technical skills. Very few
jobs or exciting opportunities are obtained simply because of
technical skills or job performance. Often there are many qualified
candidates for one opportunity, and the person hiring looks for
something more than just technical skills. People who advance are
seen as people who are good *corporate citizens.* The quality and
style of your commitment to your company—how visible you are
at your company, how others perceive you, the quality of your
participation in the community—determines what kind of corporate
citizen you are.

Some people scoff and call this politics, saying that this is unfair
or refusing to participate. But, in fact, being part of a corporate
community is just as important as doing your job. And being a
good corporate citizen involves your general character, your
willingness to see beyond your job to what is needed by the
whole organization, and your ability to be helpful to others.
These personal qualities in many work situations are as important
as technical ones in determining advancement. In fact, as you
progress in any organization, human skills—the ability to create
good working relationships—become as important as technical
skills.

Exercise 1: Enlarging My Job

Take a few moments now to brainstorm some of the new skills, challenges, experiences, projects, good ideas, assignments, and responsibilities you could take on to enlarge your job and write them down. Try to think creatively. Sometimes the ways to enlarge your job lie in going beyond the boundaries of your current job description.

Where Can You Go? The next area to explore is where you can go as you develop your career. If you don't have a destination, then you cannot move from where you are. We have been conditioned to see only one direction for career advancement: *moving up* to a higher level position. However, since there are fewer positions at each higher level of the organization, that cannot work for everyone. Must the people who do not advance simply move on to other organizations? To compound the situation, with the flattening of the organization there are fewer steps up available for everyone. People tend to *plateau,* that is, to remain at roughly the same organizational level for longer times than in the past. Few people actually face a career of continually moving up. Sooner or later, most people will reach their plateau, where the opportunities to advance are severely limited. Is this the end of the line for career development? Or are there other options?

In fact, there are many directions in which you can develop your career. The next challenge for you may not lie in moving upward. Some of the other options for career development are represented graphically in Figure 1 and described on the next page.

Moving Across ◀•▶

In a flat organization, most job changes are lateral—that is, moves to different jobs at the same level. Why move laterally? There are good reasons:

▶ To gain new experience and skills

▶ To get away from a job that has become routine

▶ The organization needs help somewhere else

▶ Your job is no longer as important to the organization

▶ To get a better understanding of the whole organization

Figure 1. Career Development Options

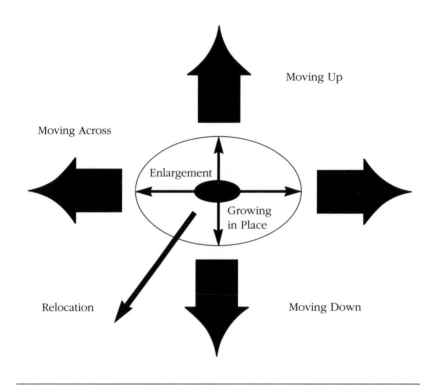

As you can see, some of the reasons for moving laterally have to do with your feelings about your job and your own growth and learning, and some have to do with what the organization needs.

People who are successful at work and who are valuable to the organization today tend to be those who are not narrowly specialized and who have a broad mix of skills. This is the era of the *utility fielder.*

To explore whether a lateral move would be useful to you, think about what you want to learn and the skills you want to develop. What type of job might broaden your skills and experience? Also, consider what new challenges you might want to seek.

Moving Down

How could it possibly be part of career development to move down? This doesn't have to mean that you have failed at your job. Sometimes, for example, a person takes a promotion and finds he or she doesn't like it.

Or you may find that the things you liked to do are no longer part of the job. It is not a disgrace to move down. Another possible reason for moving down, or realignment, is to develop a new skill or find a new challenge. In the long run, you may want to learn something new badly enough to be willing to move down in order to take a new opportunity. For example, a downward move to an up-and-coming department or work group might not be so bad. Don't rule out strategic downward moves in your career development.

Growing in Place ⊙

Sometimes the job you want can be the one you have. What you need to do is to change the job you have. In fact, job enlargement is the career development option for perhaps half the work force either before or until another job is open or they are prepared for a new one. Job enrichment is when you add new challenges or changes to the job you have. You may be able to take on a new assignment or develop a new skill where you are.

The initiative for job enrichment can lie within you. If you see something that needs doing or a new task, you can suggest it to your manager; volunteer if you like. Take some time and think about your own job. Are there some ways that you might develop by enlarging or changing it? This is something to discuss with your manager, but not before you put in some creative thinking. Enlarging or enriching your job is also a way to build new skills that prepare you for the next step.

Relocation ✔

Relocation is leaving the company. Sometimes you get to the point where you feel stalled, frustrated, or unrewarded in your organization. Your manager may not see you as you see yourself, or the organization may not have the opportunities or wherewithal to reward you the way you think you ought to be. Or there may be a deep conflict between what you want to do and what the organization needs.

These may be times when the best solution is to leave the organization. However, before you leave, the best strategy is to make your feelings known and try to see if there are other possibilities that exist inside the organization to get what you want.

Growth, Risk, and Learning. Career development is like other types of growth: It only happens when you take action, seek information, and create opportunity. Many of the tasks in career development, perhaps most of them, will be a little scary. Calling strangers, seeking information, learning new skills, taking on a new job—all of these involve creating some stress taking risks. A risk is doing something that you can fail at. You take a risk because of the possibility that you can gain from it. Career development involves risking change, trying things that are new and that take you beyond your comfort zone into new territory. As you stretch beyond your comfort zone, you learn, grow, and expand your capability. You can expect that you will feel anxiety and resistance to doing the tasks you set for yourself. While you have to overcome your resistance, you cannot expect it to go away.

You have explored your own goals and skills. Now, look outside yourself at the community of your company. Where do you see yourself moving? Keep in mind the career development options described above. Think about the next reasonable step for you. Is it a move up, down, sideways, or out?

Exercise 2: Your Job Options

Answer the following questions in relation to the next year. You may want to refer back to your answers in the self-assessment section. Let these questions be a springboard for you to reflect on the options you might have at your company.

What skills would you like to develop?

Which of these skills do you sense is most important or valuable to your company?

What direction of career development is most relevant to your goals: in place, up, across, down, or out?

Which is the second most relevant or likely direction for your career development?

What specific new jobs or types of work are your goal?

New Skills: Creating a Learning Plan. Education and learning are a life-long process. Every year you will want to learn new skills and expand your capacity. You can't coast because your company will always be changing and demanding a higher level of skill and productivity. The best way to develop job security is to develop your personal skills.

The key to career development is to develop additional skills or to deepen the skills you have. You can do that by taking advantage of educational opportunities inside your company as well as outside.

Exercise 3: Your Training/Learning Options

Think of the skills and capacities that are most important to you.

List them below in order of their importance or priority to you.

Check the training courses at your company. Which ones are most relevant to the development of these skills? Be specific.

Consider the other skills you want to develop and what courses or opportunities are available in your home community. (You may need to do some research to answer this.)

Is there a degree or certificate program that is relevant to your goals?

Networking: Exploring Resources. Networking is meeting people and gathering information from them that will help you do your work more effectively and make better career choices. It is probably the most important career development activity you can be involved in. You learn firsthand about areas you are interested in and meet people who might hire you.

Any company is a large community and you cannot expect your manager to know everything that happens there. Your manager may know of some opportunities, but you are the one who must seek them out. Networking is the systematic seeking out of resources and information.

You meet people and get information from them about the work you're considering. It's like being a detective, but your client is yourself. Then you compare what you hear with your interests, values, skills, and needs.

Exercise 4: Networking

In career development, you want to learn as much as you can about the parts of your company where you may want to work. Also, you want to seek people out to let them know what you want. Then, when something comes up, they will know to talk to you.

1. Start by making a list of all the people you know at your company. List the people in your work group first, then all the friends, acquaintances, and people you have met and worked with in other departments. It may be a very long list.

2. Then begin an informal exploration of options. Get together with people you know to talk in general about what they are doing, what you want to know, and your own needs or goals. Don't be too focused, as your goal is just to gather general information.

3. Set up some specific targets—jobs, parts of the company, or possibilities that may be relevant to your goals. If you don't know somebody in this area, find somebody who does. Or look in the phone book. One of the expectations of working at your company is that you are expected to be available to other people who are seeking career development information. Make a list of people you would like to know in the areas of interest to you. These people might include the managers in areas that hold interest for you or even the person who does the kind of work you would like.

4. Set up a series of information interviews with people on your list. Start with people you know to build up your confidence and to get used to the process. This interview is a short meeting designed to help you gather information about their job to aid your career development. For the interview, you might ask a person how they do their work, what skills they use, what they look for in employees, the challenges and drawbacks of the work, what previous job experience and education helps them do the job, and how a person can prepare for that position.

   Here are some guidelines for information interviewing:

Make them on your own time.

Make it clear that you are not job hunting, but gathering
   career development information.

Set clear, short time boundaries (e.g., 30 to 60 minutes).

Prepare what you want to ask.

Send a thank-you note.

Write down what you learned.

Don't bring a resume. You can send one later if it is
   relevant and there is a real job possibility.

5.   Keep good notes on who you meet and what you learn. Follow up
     when appropriate, and stay in touch with key resources. Expand
     your list with new contacts suggested by your resources.

6.   Don't network only inside of your company. You can learn a lot
     from people in other companies and get new ideas and new
     perspectives. Seek out people outside the company, even in other
     fields and areas of work. The process of career development
     involves casting your net wide at first before you narrow it down.

Making Yourself Visible: Creating Opportunity. To find new opportunities,
you will need to make yourself visible at your company. Not only will you
be seeking out people in your networking, but you need to put yourself
out in other ways.

People who are visible are considered for new opportunities. You can
make yourself visible by doing things that are seen by others.

▶   Volunteer for community and service activities. These bring
    you in contact with many people in the company.

▶   Get a great new idea and sell it to your company. Employees
    who come up with creative, breakthrough ideas become
    company heroes.

▶   Volunteer for jobs that bring you to other work groups, such
    as being part of task forces or working on publications.

▶   Don't eat and spend time only with the same group of
    co-workers. Expand your social group.

▶   Ask for help and seek out people to gather information for
    projects you are doing.

▶   Be helpful to others, even if it means going out of your way.

Mentors: Career Guides. Mentors are people who are somewhat ahead of you in the organization, who help you develop your career. They often create opportunities for you. When a mentor advances, he or she usually takes some people into the new job.

How do you find a mentor? People develop mentors in several ways:

▶ Do something impressive or special that is noticed.

▶ Be especially helpful to someone above you.

▶ Find something that a person or the company needs, propose it, and do it.

▶ Be friendly and get to know people.

▶ Be curious, seek information, and share your ideas.

Stage 3: Create a Plan. In Stage 3 you sift through everything you've learned about yourself and about the organization and make your career development plan. You return again to your personal dreams and goals and set some specific targets, keeping in mind what you have learned about what's possible. With concrete, specific long- and short-term goals, select some activities that promise you help in reaching them.

▶ Set your goals down on paper.

▶ Write a career description of your future, including specific activities that lead toward your goal.

▶ Meet with your manager to complete your plan. Your manager may provide some new slants or insights and help you develop it further.

At this stage you draw on the help of your manager as a person who knows you well to help you make the choices about your career plan. You may need additional help or counseling if you are a Wanderer or a Spanner.

Stage 4: Take Action. Your plan now depends on the strength and clarity of your commitment. It can get lost as you pursue the details of your everyday work, or you can keep your future constantly before you. The key is finding activities every day that advance your goals. Break your plan down into key activities for every week, and always be on the lookout for new possibilities.

Pursue your plan. This may involve taking courses or training, getting an advanced degree, developing new skills, or preparing yourself for a new job. You may seek new experiences on the job with the guidance of your manager. Begin to let others know what you want.

Stage 5: Evaluate the Outcome. As you implement your plan, you need to keep asking yourself, How does this feel? Have you made the right choice? Are you satisfied? If you answer yes, then your task is to keep up with changes. Remember, while you may be satisfied, over time your feelings can change, and certainly your company can change, so you need to keep checking in.

If your answer is no, then you need to go back to an earlier stage of the planning process and begin again. When you go back to an earlier stage of career planning, you will discover some new information about yourself and your environment and perhaps investigate another choice or direction.

A Career Development Discussion

Now you may want to have a career development discussion with your manager or mentor. You have done a lot of self-assessment work on your own. Now you will draw on the experience and perspective of your manager as a guide and resource to help you develop your potential at your company.

The meeting should not be a major source of anxiety. It is not meant to be a performance evaluation or assessment meeting. In fact, you are in control of the information you share and the outcome. However, the more candid and open you are, the more useful the meeting can be.

Your manager or mentor is a sounding board, a facilitator, and a coach for you. He or she will not do your work and does not know everything. In the meeting you will very likely come up with information to seek or new activities to undertake to reach your goals. Be open to what you can learn, and be ready to do the work.

3

· · · · · · · · ·

Using the Strong Interest Inventory and the Myers-Briggs Type Indicator ® Together in Career Counseling

JEAN M. KUMMEROW

Introduction

"I'd like to take some tests to help me decide what I should be." Most career counselors have heard that kind of statement (wish!) before, a statement that implies a view of career counseling as the narrow process of finding a job (as soon as possible) and tests as omniscient in that process. The essence of career counseling is much broader. Counselors help clients understand themselves and the career search process as well as identify a career direction for themselves; they learn a process that they may have to or want to use over and over again in the future. Yes, tests can be helpful in considering different careers and in pointing out client styles, but they are only a small part of the process.

This chapter will look at the role of two of the most widely used tests in career counseling, the *Myers-Briggs Type Indicator®* (MBTI®) and the *Strong Interest Inventory,* and point out some strategies in using the instruments separately and together. This will not be an introduction to either instrument, although some resources for reviewing the basics are included.

To recall why these tests are used in the career counseling process, keep in mind that they are systematic and efficient means of gathering data and summarizing. They give information on personality style and interests.

They have the advantage of being oriented toward the positive and are more objective and less biased in the way they look at clients. They may confirm what clients already know about themselves as well as point to new directions and give more to think about. In other words, they save time and give some good information, but they do not give the answers.

When discussing these instruments with clients, it's best to avoid using the word *test* because that implies a right or wrong. Both instruments are value-free and point to patterns of differences that are part of our personality. Neither one measures abilities.

The Two Instruments

Strong Interest Inventory

The *Strong* is an empirically based measure of vocational interests. It provides an assessment of an individual's occupational interests by comparing that person's interests with the interests of people happily employed in a wide variety of occupations. It was carefully constructed to take a broad range of familiar occupational tasks and day-to-day activities and match responses on these items to those of people in the sample occupations. It consists of three sections: the *General Occupational Themes* (based on John Holland's theory of vocational types), the *Basic Interest Scales* (23 scales of common activities), and the *Occupational Scales* (207 occupational comparisons). The General Occupational Themes, or Holland codes, are classified as follows:

▶ Realistic (R)—outdoors, technical, mechanical interests

▶ Investigative (I)—scientific, inquiring, analytical interests

▶ Artistic (A)—dramatic, musical, self-expressive interests

▶ Social (S)—helping, guiding, group-oriented interests

▶ Enterprising (E)—business, persuasive, political interests

▶ Conventional (C)—methodical, organized, clerical interests

Since specific career titles are generated, this instrument has a direct translation into possible careers for the client. It is generally easy to understand, since most of the categories and occupations fit with our everyday understandings of the terms. It has a sixth-grade reading level and usually requires 20 to 30 minutes for the client to complete.

Some basic resources on the *Strong* include *Introduction to the Strong for Career Counselors* (Levin, 1991), *The Strong User's Guide* (Hansen, 1984), *Career Development Guide for Use with the Strong Interest Inventory* (Brew, 1987), chapter 10 of the *Manual for the Strong Interest Inventory* (Hansen & Campbell, 1985), and *Introduction to the Strong in Organizational Settings* (Hirsh & Vessey, 1987). The Brew guide is particularly useful in providing a methodology to identify the Holland codes and to verify that code's fit to a client.

Myers-Briggs Type Indicator

The MBTI is based on Carl Jung's theory of behavior patterns related to how individuals perceive information and make decisions. Four preference dimensions are included:

▶ How an individual energizes: external focus with *Extraverts (E)* or internal focus with *Introverts (I)*

▶ How an individual perceives information: *Sensing (S)* through attention to the details and what is or *Intuitive (N)* through attention to the big picture and what might be

▶ How decisions get made: *Thinking (T)* through logical analysis or *Feeling (F)* through person-centered values

▶ Lifestyle: with *Judgers (J)* preferring to reach closure and make decisions or *Perceivers (P)* preferring to stay open to options

It results in sixteen types and provides general personality descriptions and styles. The focus with the MBTI is broader and toward more general aspects of personality. It takes more time to generate specific career options since it is more a general assessment tool. It has an eighth-grade reading level and takes an average of 20 to 30 minutes to complete.

With the MBTI, the following resources are helpful: Chapter 5 of the *Manual: A Guide to the Development and Use of the Myers-Briggs Type Indicator* (Myers & McCaulley, 1985), *Verifying Your Type Preferences Worksheet and Leader's Guide* (Kummerow, 1987), *Introduction to Type* (Myers, 1987), *Introduction to Type in Organizations* (2nd ed.; Hirsh & Kummerow, 1990), *Gifts Differing* (Myers, 1980, 1990) and *LIFETypes* (Hirsh & Kummerow, 1989). The first two resources are particularly useful in helping clients verify their *best fit* or *true type*. That is the type that best describes them, which is not necessarily the same as the type shown on their MBTI results.

**Table 1. Relationships Between the Occupations in a Holland
General Occupational Theme and the MBTI Preference Scales**

Occupations in the Theme	Sex	MBTI Preferences
Realistic	Males	I, S, T
	Females	T
Investigative	Males	I, N, J
	Females	I, N, T
Artistic	Males	N, F, P
	Females	N, P
Social	Males	E, S, F
	Females	E, N, P
Enterprising	Males	E, S
	Females	E, T, F
Conventional	Males	E, S, J
	Females	S, T, J

Note: This table includes several studies mostly of college students. In order for a preference to appear in this table, the correlation had to be significant at a .05 level or better, and over 50 percent of the occupations in that Holland code had to contain that letter. Results may seem contradictory, such as the female Enterprising occupations containing a majority of T's in one study and F's in another study. Overall, correlations are generally low; with the sample sizes used in some of these studies, correlations as low as .07 are significant at $p \leq .05$. Incidentally, the highest correlation reported in the MBTI *Manual* is .52 between Sensing and female farmers.

Correlations Between the Two Instruments

These instruments appear to be measuring different aspects of personality. While there are correlations between the two and in the directions expected, the correlations are generally small. Table 1 contains a summary of the general trends when correlating the MBTI preference scales and the occupations in a particular General Occupational Theme. For additional information on the correlations between the instruments, see sources such as Tables 7.8 and 11.1 in the MBTI *Manual* (Myers & McCaulley, 1985), Nelson (1986), and Dillon and Weissman (1987).

Both instruments are used in career counseling because they add to the picture of understanding our clients. In this chapter I'll describe different ways to use the instruments in this process and how to integrate them when possible.

Career Development Counseling

To focus the career development process, I'm going to use the stages outlined by Jaffe and Scott in their chapter in this volume:

▶ Stage 1: Assess yourself

▶ Stage 2: Explore possibilities

▶ Stage 3: Create a plan

▶ Stage 4: Take action

▶ Stage 5: Evaluate the outcome

Stage 1: Assess Yourself

This first stage centers on who our clients are—their personal characteristics, interests, and abilities—and what they've already done in terms of their paid and unpaid work history and their significant avocational activities.

Personal Characteristics. Exercise 1 is a summation of the client's personal characteristics based on MBTI type (the type the client has validated as his or her most accurate description) and Holland codes (usually the top two or three themes). In completing this exercise, it is helpful to have the report forms and type and code descriptions in front of the client. Either the client or the counselor can act as the recorder in this step.

Exercise 1: Description of Self

MBTI type _____   Holland code _____

Write down key words or phrases that describe you from your understanding of your MBTI type and Holland code:

Occasionally contradictory information may surface. This was the case with an ESFJ who had an A-theme. ESFJs typically prefer structured, organized situations working with a group of compatible people. A-theme people, on the other hand, prefer freedom and spontaneity and are stifled by a great deal of structure. They often like working alone. This client found the ESFJ more descriptive of her on this issue. Incidentally, she settled on dance therapy, which combined her need for some structure and camaraderie with her artistic, creative side.

Extroversion/Introversion Combinations From Both Instruments. Another piece of personal assessment centers on the Extraversion/Introversion scores on both instruments. These scales measure different characteristics, although there is some overlap between them. On the MBTI, the E–I dimension refers to the general orientation of a person's energy. On the *Strong,* the E–I refers more to the object or recipient of the energy, particularly in a work environment. Studies reported in the MBTI *Manual*(Myers & McCaulley, 1985) show correlations of .35 to .47 between the two instruments on this E–I dimension.

The MBTI shows the preferred source and direction of energy—for the Introvert, these are inward, and for the Extravert, outward. Operating in the preferred world is more likely to be invigorating. The Extravert is likely to be out and about with people, enjoying talking things through with others. The Introvert is likely to seek privacy and quiet and reflect on his or her thoughts and ideas.

On the *Strong,* it is the recipient, or object of that energy, especially in a work setting, that is the focus of the E–I scale. On the *Strong,* the Extroverts (with scores below 45) prefer working with people. Introverts (with scores above 55) prefer working with data or things or ideas. There is also a middle group on the *Strong* (with scores of 45–55), who seem to like a mixture of people, data, things, and ideas.

Six combinations of E–I on these two instruments are possible. Let's look at those who may work as career counselors and their combinations. The MBTI Extravert/*Strong* Extrovert counselors clearly focus their energies on people, often preferring group counseling to one-on-one interactions. They prefer to be active and like to see action in their clients. They sometimes say it is difficult for them to listen since they like talking and projecting their energy outward. Regular contact with colleagues is important to them.

The MBTI Introvert/*Strong* Extrovert counselors also like to focus their energies on people, but often prefer one-on-one counseling to groups. They like to work with people and focus on people-related issues, but they can feel overloaded with people contact and need time away to recharge their energies. They often feel a need for an abrupt break from their work activities with people in order to have some time alone. They may prefer to lunch alone, for example, as well as have quiet evenings at home.

Counselors with midscores on the *Strong* emphasize a mixture of activities in their career counseling; they often work with people and ideas and report comfort with the range of activities they have for themselves. MBTI Extravert/*Strong* midscore counselors seem to spend more time in the outside world and often show more external energies. They like to talk their ideas over with people. MBTI Introvert/*Strong* midscore counselors show less external energy and like to think their ideas through by themselves. They also do not seem to need an abrupt break in activities to their quiet time that their MBTI Introvert/*Strong* Extrovert colleagues report, since part of their work day is already spent by themselves.

The MBTI Introvert/*Strong* Introvert career counselors like to control their contact with others. They feel quite comfortable reflecting on data about the job market, looking perhaps at such issues as theories of career development. They prefer brief and concise communications and often dislike going to meetings. They like to deal with the situation and the data more than the person.

The MBTI Extravert/*Strong* Introvert counselors (a rare combination in this occupation) seem to like to be out and about gathering pieces of information and ideas that would enhance their work. They think nothing of going out and visiting potential job sites, for example, but prefer to do that on their own rather than invite their colleagues along. Their energies are external but focused on things more than people.

We can help clients think through their specific E–I combination. Exercise 2 gives a possible format. Figure 1 gives an example of one client's responses to Exercise 2. This client is an introvert on the MBTI and in the middle group on the *Strong*. There may be times in each client's career development process where a return to activities that are particularly energizing are important. Referring back to this exercise at a later stage may be useful.

Exercise 2: Extraversion/Introversion

My preferred source of energy (E = external; I = internal):

Activities I do to gain energy:

My preferred recipient of energy (E = people, I = data/ideas/things, middle = both):

Activities I like to put energy into:

Figure 1. Client Responses to the E–I Combination in Exercise 2

My preferred source of energy (E = external; I = internal): *I*

Activities I do to gain energy: *Read, go on walks by myself,*
stay up alone late at night, work on a project by myself

My preferred recipient of energy (E = people, I = data/ideas/things,
middle = both): *Middle*

Activities I like to put energy into: *One-on-one meetings; researching*
things to help my clients; designing training courses, although I also
like to teach the course too. I do need some alone time each day.

Job Characteristics. A second part of self-assessment involves reviewing
the jobs clients have had in the past and how they liked them. Here we
include both paid and unpaid work. At your own discretion, you may
choose to include avocational activities, especially when a client may seem
particularly disparaging about the jobs he or she has held, but seems to
have positive experiences with hobbies. In Exercise 3, we estimate the
MBTI preferences (one or more of the preference letters) and both the
Holland codes and Basic Interest Scales from the *Strong* that clients believed were utilized in each job. Tables 2 and 3 focus on the work activities
likely to be part of the Holland codes and the MBTI preferences.

In helping your clients with Exercise 3, it is useful to have their résumés
along with Table 2 to identify their Holland codes and Table 3 for their
MBTI preferences for their work activities. Most résumés exclude unpaid
work experiences, so make sure you probe for that information as well.

Exercise 3: Job Review

Past Jobs/ Activities	How Well I Liked Them	MBTI Preferences Used	Holland Codes Used	Basic Interest Scales

Patterns I noted:

Table 2. Holland Codes and Typical Work Activities

Realistic (R)	Social (S)
Doing jobs that produce tangible results	Teaching, training
	Coaching
Operating or designing equipment or huge machines	Leading discussions
Using tools that require manual dexterity	Doing group projects

Investigative (I)	Enterprising (E)
Solving problems through thinking	Selling, purchasing
Doing scientific or laboratory work	Leading and managing people
Collecting and organizing data	Managing projects
	Chairing committees

Artistic (A)	Conventional (C)
Composing, writing	Keeping records and financial books
Decorating, designing	Making charts, graphs, and slides
Completing projects independently	Scheduling
	Organizing and maintaining office procedures

From *Career Development Guide for Use with the Strong Interest Inventory* by S. Brew, 1987, Palo Alto, CA: Consulting Psychologists Press. Copyright 1987 by Consulting Psychologists Press. Reprinted by permission.

Table 3. MBTI Preferences and Typical Work Activities

Extraverts (E)	Introverts (I)
Like variety and action	Like quiet for concentration
Are often impatient with long, slow jobs	Tend not to mind working on one project for a long time uninterruptedly
Are interested in the activities of their work and in how other people do it	Are interested in the facts and ideas behind their work
Often act quickly, sometimes without thinking	Like to think a lot before they act, sometimes without acting
When working on a task, find phone calls a welcome diversion	When concentrating on a task, find phone calls intrusive
Develop ideas by discussion	Develop ideas by reflection
Like having people around	Like working alone

Sensing Types (S)	Intuitive Types (N)
Like using experience and standard ways to solve problems	Like solving new complex problems
Enjoy applying what they have already learned	Enjoy learning a new skill more than using it
May distrust and ignore their inspirations	May follow their inspirations, good or bad
Seldom make errors of fact	May make errors of fact
Like to do things with a practical bent	Like to do things with an innovative bent
Like to present the details of their work first	Like to present an overview of their work first
Prefer continuation of what is, with fine-tuning	Prefer change, sometimes radical, to continuation of what is
Usually proceed step-by-step	Usually proceed in bursts of energy

From *Introduction to Type in Organizations* (2nd ed.) by S. K. Hirsh and J. M.Kummerow, Palo Alto, CA: Consulting Psychologists Press. Copyright 1990 by Consulting Psychologists Press. Reprinted by permission.

Table 3. MBTI Preferences and Typical Work Activities (continued)

Thinking Types (T)	Feeling Types (F)
Use logical analysis to reach conclusions	Use values to reach conclusions
Can work without harmony	Work best in harmony with others
May hurt people's feelings without knowing it	Enjoy pleasing people, even in unimportant things
Tend to decide impersonally, sometimes paying insufficient attention to people's wishes	Often let decisions be influenced by their own and other people's likes and dislikes
Tend to be firm-minded and can give criticism when appropriate	Tend to be sympathetic and dislike, even avoid, telling people unpleasant things
Look at the principles involved in the situation	Look at the underlying values in the situation
Feel rewarded when a job is done well	Feel rewarded when people's needs are met

Judging Types (J)	Perceiving Types (P)
Work best when they can plan their work and follow their plan	Enjoy flexibility in work
Like to get things settled and finished	Like to leave things open for last-minute changes
May not notice new things that need to be done	May postpone unpleasant tasks that need to be done
Tend to be satisfied once they reach a decision on a thing, situation, or person	Tend to be curious and welcome a new light on a thing, situation, or person
Reach closure by deciding quickly	Postpone decisions while searching for options
Seek structure and schedules	Adapt well to changing situations and feel restricted without change
Use lists to prompt action or specific tasks	Use lists to remind them of all the things they have to do someday

One INFP with an A–theme recalled several summers in which he worked at construction—one summer he liked the job, the second summer he did not. The second summer he felt the job emphasized Sensing on the MBTI, the Realistic Holland code, and Mechanical Activities under the Basic Interest Scale. For the first summer, he listed Intuitive–Feeling for the MBTI preferences. On the *Strong,* he listed Artistic for the Holland code and Art on the Basic Interest Scale. That summer he was working on an historic renovation project where he felt somewhat creative in being able to discover and recreate the way a building had been in the past. That made all the difference to him as to how well he liked the job and provided a good clue for his career path into specialized historic renovation. Incidentally, his brothers also held construction jobs, but felt differently about them than he did. His ESTP brother enjoyed the construction work for the day-to-day activity, the camaraderie it provided him, and the enjoyment of working with his hands. Thus, he emphasized the Extraverted–Sensing preferences on the MBTI and the Realistic code on the *Strong.* Their INTJ brother totally disliked construction work, quitting after several weeks. He found the day-to-day work tedious and the camaraderie draining.

Unpaid work often gets the short shrift in looking at careers. Home-makers may emphasize many of the MBTI preferences, depending on how they go about their jobs. One may use extraversion, joining up with other neighborhood parents and children while another may use more introversion, working on chores alone. One may use sensing, paying much attention to all the details of daily life, and another may use intuition more, always experimenting with a new recipe or taking a new course with the children or going on an adventure of a field trip.

The Holland code of a homemaker is likely Social. However, there are any number of basic interest scales that could be identified here, depending on how the work is done: Domestic Arts, Teaching, Social Service, Mechanical Activities, Art, Adventure, and so forth. It is important to avoid stereotypes in looking at unpaid work activities. Volunteer activities and hobbies may provide valuable self-assessment information.

In summary, this stage provides clients with the opportunity to reflect, in a systematic way, on who they are and what they've done. Patterns often begin to emerge, and these can be used in the later stages. For some clients, this stage can provide some needed emotional venting, especially if they have been led to career counseling through circumstances beyond their control. It can also begin to focus clients on their strengths, what they have liked in the past, and the depth of their experiences, which all can be used to build a new career.

Stage 2: Explore Possibilities

In this stage, clients identify some possibilities for themselves in the world of work. The MBTI and the *Strong* can be particularly useful in pointing clients in new directions and helping them think of specific occupations to explore. Several resources help advance this stage, including the MBTI *Manual* (Myers & McCaulley, 1985), the *Strong-Hansen Occupational Guide* (Hansen, 1987), the *Dictionary of Holland Occupational Codes* (Gottfredson, Holland, & Ogawa, 1982), and the *Atlas of Type Tables* (Macdaid, McCaulley, & Kainz, 1986). There are two parts to this stage: first, helping clients identify as many possibilities as possible; and second, helping clients narrow down those possibilities into realistic choices.

There are dangers in this stage of sticking too closely to the test data and thus limiting clients unnecessarily or of being overly concerned about apparent contradictions in the data. If a client has an interest in a particular job and it does not come up on the inventories, still include it on the possibilities list. This is their opportunity to add their dream occupations. (They may find themselves eliminating those when they become practical again!)

The Possibilities. Exercise 4 provides a format for recording the various possibilities generated by the two instruments and, of course, by the client's dreams. With the *Strong,* the process begins with noting the occupational scales on which the client scored at least moderately similar or higher. (For clients with flat or depressed profiles, use the ten highest scores on the occupational scales, even though this means moving into the midrange scores.) This process also involves extrapolating to other occupations based on similar Holland codes. The purpose is to look at as many choices as possible initially, narrowing those choices down in later stages.

The process with the MBTI focuses on available career information from Appendix D of the MBTI *Manual* and on additional resources from the *Atlas of Type Tables.* Career information by preferences and type are available from these sources.

Exercise 4: Possibilities Suggested by the Instruments

Job Possibility	Source	
	Strong	MBTI

As an illustration, let's look at one client, a 30-year-old ISFJ woman working in a sales capacity in investment banking. Her Holland code was SCR. Figure 2 illustrates how this process worked for her.

Figure 2. A Possibilities Example

Job Possibility	Source	
	Strong	MBTI
Horticulture worker	√	
Farmer	√	
Vocational agriculture teacher	√	
Physical therapist	√	√
Dietitian	√	√
Chef	√	
Flight attendant	√	
English teacher	√	
Foreign language teacher	√	
Social science teacher	√	
Elementary teacher	√	√
Special education teacher	√	
YWCA director	√	
Home economics teacher	√	
Beautician	√	
Florist	√	
Food service manager	√	
Secretary	√	√
Banker	√	
Philologist (linguist)	√	
Physical therapist assistant	√	
Library clerk	√	
Director of state historical society	√	
Interpreter for the deaf	√	
Career guidance technician	√	
Aide to the blind	√	
Preschool teacher		√
Speech therapy teacher		√
Librarian		√
Archivist		√
Curator		√
Reading teacher		√
Nursing administrator		√
Career counselor	√	
Braille transcriber	√	

We began by listing all of the occupations on our client's *Strong* in which she was *at least moderately similar*. These included horticulture worker, farmer, vocational agricultural teacher, physical therapist, dietitian, chef, flight attendant, English teacher, foreign language teacher, social science teacher, elementary teacher, special education teacher, YWCA director, home economics teacher, beautician, florist, food service manager, secretary, and banker.

Our next step was to turn to the *Dictionary of Holland Occupational Codes* and look for occupations with Holland Codes that were the same as or similar to hers, in this case SCR. We found such occupations as philologist (linguist), physical therapist assistant, library clerk, director of state historical society, and office copy selector. We added several of these to the list of occupations to explore. We then expanded the search to include the SEC code, since Enterprising did come up on several occupations in which she had worked successfully. Occupations such as interpreter for the deaf, career guidance technician, and aide to the blind were added to the list. Educational level of these jobs is irrelevant at this point, since we are simply generating possibilities and may extrapolate to a higher level job based on the initial possibility.

Next, we turned to the MBTI *Manual* to the ISFJ list of occupations in Appendix D. Keep in mind that these are samples of convenience, not random samples, so the lists may be somewhat limited as a result. Looking at about the top quarter of the occupations is most useful, since these are the occupations most likely to attract people of that type. The top quarter represents a rather crude self-selection ratio, a procedure explained more fully in Chapter 7 of the MBTI *Manual*. Occupations such as preschool teacher, speech therapy teacher, librarian, archivist, curator, elementary teacher, reading teacher, library attendant, and nursing administrator appear to attract ISFJs. A look at the *Atlas of Type Tables* did not add additional occupations.

With this long list, it then became important for the client to do research on the possibilities, so we initially turned to the *Strong-Hansen Occupational Guide*. In reading more detailed descriptions of the occupations listed on the *Strong*, our client was able to eliminate several because with more information, she found they did not appeal to her. Based on the information contained in a section of the *Guide*, which includes occupations related to those listed in the *Strong*, she added career counselor and braille transcriber to her list. (Even more information on occupations can be found in the *Dictionary of Occupational Titles* [U.S. Department of Labor, 1977, 1987]; this client was feeling overwhelmed by the possibilities and did not look further.)

In conclusion (and moving to stages 3 and 4), after giving considerable thought to this information and her lifestyle desires, she ultimately decided to concentrate specifically on elementary school teaching with a specialty

Table 4. Strategies to Deal With the Occupations Suggested by the MBTI and *Strong*

	Occupation Similar to Interests Based on Strong Scores	Occupation Not Similar to Interests Based on Strong Scores
Occupation Attractive to MBTI Type	A good bet; continue exploring (1)	Explore nature of *Strong* sample; find similar occupation with more compatible interests (3)
Occupation Not Attractive to MBTI Type	Explore how an "unusual" type would do the job (2)	Check out why client is interested; this may not be a good choice (4)

Note: Special thanks to Dr. Allen Hammer, Senior Product Developer, Consulting Psychologists Press, Palo Alto, CA, for conceptualizing this model.

in reading. She talked with teachers in the field and checked into further educational requirements. Two years after our initial meetings, she had enrolled in a Master's degree program in education, had a baby and volunteered often at the child's daycare, and began applying for jobs to work as an aide in a school to gain more experience.

Integration of the Two Instruments. While clients will have their thoughts and feelings about each occupation they place on the list in Exercise 4, they often need guidance on which to explore first and what type of information to seek. Table 4 illustrates the possible combinations of the two instruments and strategies to handle the information generated.

When the Instruments Agree. The best bets to explore first (and further) are those occupations with scores of at least moderately similar and where many people of the client's same type self-select into that occupation (see category 1 in Table 4). That was the case with the ISFJ Social-theme woman who chose elementary education. Both instruments included this occupation, and her strategy then was to gather even more information.

However, keep in mind that type and interests do not tell all. The additional information gathered may show that the career choice is actually inappropriate. For example, one client scored similar to people in accounting and had the type preference of ISTJ, a seemingly good match. But on a test of mathematical aptitude he scored low. That information helped round out the picture that accounting was not likely to be a good choice. Another individual with the type preference of ESTJ and interests similar to many managerial jobs (store manager, Chamber of Commerce executive, restaurant manager, etc.) had very low scores on another instrument relating to dominance and assertiveness and, indeed, did not display these characteristics in his behavior. Thus, he would have had a difficult time being successful in those positions. Competencies in addition to personality and interests are important to consider. (See the Mirabile chapter in this volume.)

When the Instruments Disagree. Another possible combination (see category 2 in Table 4) is when the *Strong* points out an occupation of similar interest, but few people of that type self-select into the specific occupation. An example of this is an ESTJ psychologist whose tested interests are similar to psychologists.* In general, ESTJs are more likely to be concrete and practical and to encourage action as well as reflection in their clients. ESTJ psychologists might develop very concrete step-by-step treatment programs for clients to follow, and this approach may appeal to some types of clients. Indeed, you are reading an example of that in this chapter. As an ESTJ (with an SEC Holland code), I break career counseling into stages or steps and try to make sure I cover all of them. Admittedly I do not use every one of the exercises in this chapter with all my clients, but I do cover the topics emphasizing some in more depth.

When this combination of similar interests but different personality occurs in clients, it might be wise to look at the usual practice of that occupation and then at how someone of that type may differ in style. Often a pioneering role can be played by that individual because of his or her differences, but that person needs to be prepared for the feelings of isolation as well.

Another possibility is for the MBTI to suggest some occupations that the client wants to explore, but for the *Strong* not to show similar interests in that occupation (see category 3 in Table 4). At this point, the next step is for the counselor and client to do some more exploration regarding the specific composition of the *Strong* sample and the specific job description that was surveyed.

To illustrate the composition of the *Strong* sample's impact on the results, consider the example of an ISFJ male interested in elementary school teaching. His MBTI type seems attracted to the occupation. Yet his specific *Strong* results did not place him in the "similar" range on male elementary teacher. In examining the career paths of male elementary

---

*This is my pattern. I do feel different from most psychologists and found counselor training to be trying, but I have evolved into a niche of psychology (testing, teaching, career counseling, and writing practical materials) that does feel comfortable.

teachers in the *Strong* sample, many move to administrative positions. He expressed no interest in that particular career path. He did score in the "similar" range on female elementary teacher; the more typical career path for females in this *Strong* sample is to maintain their classroom ties. Thus, by examining the nature of the sample, additional information was gathered to confirm that elementary teaching was likely to be a satisfying career.

To see the impact of the specific job description, let's look at what one INTP did with her results. She noted pharmacist as an occupation attractive to her type, but her scores on pharmacist were not in the "similar" range. In examining the sample of pharmacists in the *Strong,* a major job activity of the sample was dispensing, an activity that did not hold particular appeal to this client. She was more interested in the research aspects of pharmacy, such as the effects of drugs on memory (and indeed had a high score on medical science). She chose a career path that took her into the laboratory, researching drugs to treat Alzheimer's disease.

These two illustrations make this process look relatively simplistic, but it may not be. Searching for occupations with more compatible interests is the goal. This involves extrapolating based on the information you have, and sometimes it's difficult to find just the right combination. Even if the client decides on an occupation with dissimilar interests, they simply need to be able to fashion a statement like this: "I understand my interests may be different, but given other factors in my life, that's the occupation I want."

When Neither Inventory Suggests the Occupation. A final combination is that of a client who expresses a personal interest in an occupation but does not show this in his or her test results. In other words, people of the same type do not often self-select into that occupation, nor does the client share similar interests with those happily employed in that particular occupation (see category 4 in Table 4). In exploring these cases, there is often a family message to enter the career, perhaps taking over the family business or carrying on the tradition of becoming a physician. Much reality testing is needed for these clients so that if they do choose the particular occupation, at least they go in with their eyes open. It would be inappropriate to eliminate any occupation on the basis of test scores only.

Finding The Realistic Possibilities. Exercise 5 is designed to narrow the focus of career possibilities. Clients are not to be concerned at this point about educational or skill requirements. They are to work on only column 1, "Possible Jobs," first. All jobs that still hold some interest after discussing them and doing some preliminary research from Exercise 4 are listed in Exercise 5 in column 1. Clients may have ideas of what additional information they need (e.g., education requirements, salary ranges, and occupational outlook) which is recorded in column 2, and the answers they find are recorded in column 3.

Exercise 5: Some Job Possibilities to Explore Further

Possible Jobs	Additional Information Needed	Information Gathered

This exercise becomes a worksheet for the client. There are times in any career search that the client feels he or she is making no progress. By having this worksheet, it is easier to see if the client's concerns have any merit. This form also shows the progress in narrowing down the job possibilities, since as clients eliminate jobs when they have no more interest in them, they simply cross through the job title. Often, energies start to dip with this and the later stages. Referring back to Exercise 2 and encouraging clients to engage in some of the activities that energize them may help.

In summary, in this stage clients are encouraged to think big about the possibilities and also to think specifically how their type might do a particular job, especially if their type might be unusual in an occupation.

Stage 3: Create a Plan

Clients now have a great deal of information about themselves, including their personal characteristics and job possibilities. Organizing the information into goals is next, and Exercise 6 helps that process. This stage involves coming to some type of closure, and thus the MBTI scale of Judging–Perceiving comes into play.

Exercise 6: Your Plan

1. Write your career goal below. For example, identify a specific job you want or occupational fields you would like to explore or area where you want to live or hours you want to work.

    Goal:

2. Now list some *steps* to take. Your steps may involve searching for more information, completing educational requirements, writing a résumé, or whatever you feel it takes. They should be as specific as possible. For example, you may need to find out what a reading teacher really does or the educational requirements for the job or

actually apply to college or finish a training program or locate companies that have flextime, and so forth.

a.

b.

c.

d.

3. As you move toward your goal, keep track of *specific activities* in which you've participated that indicate you've used each of the eight MBTI preferences. Table 3 may refresh your memory of some activities for each preference. For example, if your goal is to explore careers in advertising, when you have gathered information on the pros and cons of that field, you would note what you have done under "Thinking."

Evidence that I have used my:

Extraversion   *Introversion*

Sensing   *Intuition*

Thinking   *Feeling*

Judging   *Perceiving*

Those with a judging function may be quite ready to start closing off options, and those with a perceiving preference may want to keep options open longer. Using either one to an extreme may short-circuit the career development process. Those who use judging too quickly may miss some possibilities. Those who use perceiving too much may become overwhelmed by the possibilities. For the perceptive, the word *plan* may be uncom-

Table 5. Problem Solving Using the Eight Preferences

Extraverts	Introverts
Use your extraversion to discuss each stage of your career planning process with others and also to move to action to implement the plan.	Use your introversion to reflect on each step along the way.

Sensors	Intuitives
Use your sensing to look at the facts of the situation—who you are, how much money you need, the type of hours you might want to work, and so on.	Use your intuition to look at all the different possibilities, what else you might do, how you might do a job in a different way to refresh yourself, and so on.

Thinkers	Feelers
Use your thinking to look at the pros and cons of each job that you consider.	Use your feeling to help you look at how much you care about each possibility and how your friends and family will react to the outcome. Don't take a job simply to please others.

Judgers	Perceivers
Use your judgment to set up a time-table to move you along.	Use your perception to ensure openness to all aspects of the career development process.

fortable because it seems confining. Thinking of plans as *options* might be helpful. Judgers may be uncomfortable without a clear decision right away and need to be reminded that their plan for the moment is to stay open to possibilities.

Using the Preferences in Problem Solving. The eight preferences on the MBTI are useful guidelines in problem solving, and the career development process is, in a sense, a "problem," albeit one with many opportunities. Making sure clients have input on each one of the preferences listed in Table 5 helps round out their planning to solve their problem more fully. Clients need to pay particular attention to the preferences that are not as natural to them, that is, the ones that are not in their type.

As an example, one client with a Bachelor's degree in Russian and a résumé with several jobs coordinating social service agencies decided her long-term goal was to be an executive housekeeper of a hotel in the Soviet Union owned by an American chain. She decided upon executive housekeeper, by the way, through her *Strong* results, and also by looking at how she was spending her time in-between jobs—that is, organizing her own home and cleaning other's homes. Her own job history did not necessarily suggest that particular occupation, but she was certainly open to it. Her MBTI type preferences are ENTJ and her Holland code is ECR. Some of the steps she listed included locating training programs in hotel and restaurant management, going to the library to look up which American hotel companies did business in the Soviet Union, and talking to people in the hotel business. These activities involved using her extraversion, introversion, and sensing preferences. She'll use the other preferences later on as well.

Stage 4: Take Action

Now it's time for clients to move to action and use the information they have gathered about themselves in the first three stages. The *process* is the key in this stage and it's important to stay focused in spite of the inevitable pitfalls. Tables 6 and 7 identify possible pitfalls based on type preferences and Holland codes.

These two tables have focused on the pitfalls to avoid as clients implement the process. Everyone is likely to feel blocked at some point. When that occurs, it may be necessary to stop and look at what is happening and use a different set of behaviors to move clients forward. For example, if a client is spending so much time contemplating and reflecting (I) on the possibilities, it may be time to ask a trusted friend to work alongside (E). If a client is being too logical and analytical (T), check out what values (F) are involved.

Exercise 7 provides the opportunity for clients to look at both the negative and positive possibilities of the job search—that is, to note their own potential pitfalls as well as what they really want in their next career, the "musts." One ISTJ with a CSE theme noted that he tended to rely only on himself and did not ask his friends and family for help. He started reaching out more. He was afraid to consider another career area, even though he was very dissatisfied in his current career in sales. He had to give himself permission to look beyond what he already knew. A "must" for him

Table 6. Potential Pitfalls for the MBTI Preferences in the Career Search Process

Extraverts	Introverts
May move to action without reflecting	May think too much and appear immobilized
May talk over the decision with too many people	May isolate self and try to solve the search in a vacuum without the input of others
May contact networks too frequently just to talk and not use resources appropriately	May not develop resources and network fully
May talk without thinking in interviews	May not project enough energy and be too quiet in interviews

Sensors	Intuitives
May see very few options	May see too many options and have difficulty focusing
May be too literal in interpretation of test results	May gloss over important details in interpreting test results
May get stuck in a rut and not act	May get stuck in the possibilities and not act
May believe all requirements in a want ad are necessary before action	May ignore crucial information in a want ad
May not want to try something new	May take great risks in searching for the new and ignore reality
In interviews, may not respond well to the "What if..." questions	In interviews, may not respond well to questions asking for specific information

Table 6. Potential Pitfalls for the MBTI Preferences in the Career Search Process (continued)

Thinkers	Feelers
May expect the process to proceed logically	May expect personal relationships to win them the job
May not weigh impact of decisions on others	May take a job to please others rather than themselves
May overintellectualize and ignore their own feelings in the process	May not have logically analyzed what they need in a job
In interviews, may appear overly task-oriented and may need to chitchat more	In interviews, may appear too personable and not as someone who gets things done

Judgers	Perceivers
May become impatient with career exploration process	May spend too much time gathering information
May define career choice too soon	May delay making career choice
May appear rigid with career goal and plan	May appear unfocused with career goals and plans
In interviews, may appear too rigid	In interviews, may appear too flexible

From The Center for the Applications of Psychological Type, Workshop Exercise. Adapted by permission.

in his future work is to find a job that feels more socially redeeming to him. He began to look at teaching business education as one possibility. He has not yet settled on a new career, which is also hard for him as a judging type, but he knows that his plan is to stay open to possibilities for at least one year before he settles on a new direction. In the meantime, he is examining his relationships with others, his values, and his personal flexibility.

Table 7. Potential Pitfalls in the Career Search Process Suggested by the Holland Codes

For **Realistic (R)** people, the process

> Appears too intangible
> Has to involve other people
> Has too much ambiguity
> Is too long-range and not here-and-now enough

For **Investigative (I)** people, the process

> Has to involve other people
> Has too much structure
> Leads to overanalysis
> Requires action rather than just thinking or observing

For **Artistic (A)** people, the process

> Requires too much action
> Leads in too many directions
> Has too much structure
> Seems too practical

For **Social (S)** people, the process

> Requires too much contemplation and time alone
> Engages our desires to help other people, not ourselves
> Needs too much objectivity
> Is associated with too much conflict

For **Enterprising (E)** people, the process

> Requires too much contemplation
> Engages our competitive and aggressive characteristics
>   ("I can get a better job before you can")
> Becomes too all-consuming
> Is so challenging that we forget the purpose of doing it

For **Conventional (C)** people, the process

> Feels too ambiguous
> Has too little structure
> Focuses more on self than the job
> Demands too much creativity rather than tradition

Exercise 7: The Positives and Negatives: My Pitfalls and Musts

Identify possible pitfalls and also what you believe "must" be present in your new job/career.

Pitfalls:

Musts:

Eventually the action in this stage leads to some choices and results. However, the timetable for each person may differ, given their circumstances and perhaps even given their personality. There seems to be some evidence, for example, that introverts who have been outplaced take longer (over a month more) to find jobs than extraverts (Vacarro, 1988).

Stage 5: Evaluate Outcome

At this point, clients may want to recycle back to the self-assessment stage and review their MBTI and *Strong* results. Have them revisit the results of Exercises 1 through 3. How do the choices in the later stages fit with who the client is as a person? The question becomes, Can I live with this job and its accompanying lifestyle? It is helpful at this point to double-check.

Use of the Dominant Preference. First, does the particular job allow clients to use their dominant preferences? Table 8 identifies the dominant needs for the 16 types. Clients can ask themselves how they will be able to utilize their dominant process in their job. The activities listed for each dominant preference should be present in that job for maximum satisfaction.

Preferred Work Environments. Second, review the client's preferred work environment to see how it fits with his or her type. Table 9 looks at the work environments preferred by each one of the sixteen types. Ask the question, In what ways does your job fit your type's preferred work setting?

A third check is to have clients look at Table 10 and review their Holland codes and the work settings associated with each. What is the fit?

Table 8. The Dominant Process and Work Activities

Sensing ISTJ, ISFJ, ESTP, ESFP	Intuition INTJ, INFJ, ENTP, ENFP
Recognize the pertinent facts	Recognize new possibilities
Apply experience to problems	Supply ingenuity to problems
Notice what needs attention	See how to prepare for the future
Keep track of essentials	Watch for new essentials
Handle problems with realism	Tackle new problems with zest

Thinking ISTP, INTP, ESTJ, ENTJ	Feeling ISFP, INFP, ESFJ, ENFJ
Be good at analysis	Be good at empathizing
Find flaws in advance	Forecast how others will feel
Hold consistently to a policy	Allow for extenuating circumstances
Weigh "the law and the evidence"	Be aware of values
Stand firm against opposition	Appreciate each person's contributions

From *Introduction to Type in Organizations* (2nd ed.) by S. K. Hirsh and J. M. Kummerow, 1990, Palo Alto, CA: Consulting Psychologists Press. Copyright 1990 by Consulting Psychologists Press. Reprinted by permission.

But Nothing's Perfect. The question often asked is, What do I do if after all this, there is no perfect job for me? This is the case for nearly everyone, and some compensations and compromises get made. For example, clients may find leisure pursuits to help balance their work lives. For some, their avocational life may become even more important than their vocational life. The INFP artistic person (A-theme) who works as a typist (C-theme) may find that in her spare time she writes poetry, attends concerts and plays, and volunteers as a guide in the local art museum.

For some, it is a matter of finding a job that puts them in contact with similar people, type-wise and/or Holland code-wise. The enterprising salesperson (E-theme) with medical interests (I-theme) may sell medical products to those in hospital settings. Some others find that they change jobs often and move from interest to interest as a way to satisfy themselves. This is more likely the case for Intuitive-Perceptive types on the MBTI.

Table 9. Preferred Work Environments for Each Type

ISTJ	ISFJ
Attracts hardworking people focused on facts and results	Attracts conscientious people working on well-structured tasks
Provides security	Provides security
Rewards a steady pace	Clearly structured
Structured	Calm and quiet
Task-oriented	Efficient
Orderly	Allows for privacy
Allows privacy for uninterrupted work	Service-oriented

ISTP	ISFP
Attracts action-oriented people focused on the immediate situation	Attracts cooperative people quietly enjoying their work
Project-oriented	Allows for private space
Unconstrained by rules	Has people who are compatible
Provides many new immediate problems to solve	Flexible
	Aesthetically appealing
Allows for hands-on experience	People-oriented
Action-oriented	Includes courteous co-workers
Fosters independence	

ESTP	ESFP
Attracts lively, results-oriented people who value firsthand experience	Attracts energetic and easygoing people focused on present realities
Unbureaucratic	Lively
Allows time for fun	Action-oriented
Provides for flexibility in doing the job	Includes people who are adaptable
Technically-oriented	Harmonious
Physically attractive	People-intensive
Responsive to the needs of the moment	Attractive

Table 9. Preferred Work Environments for Each Type (continued)

ESTJ	**ESFJ**
Attracts hardworking people focused on getting the job done	Attracts conscientious, cooperative people oriented toward helping others
Task-oriented	Goal-oriented people and systems
Organized	Organized
Structured	Friendly
Provides stability and predictability	Includes people who are appreciative
Focused on efficiency	Has people who are sensitive
Rewards meeting goals	Operates on facts

INFJ	**INTJ**
Attracts people strongly focused on ideals that make a difference to human well-being	Attracts decisive, intellectually challenging people focused on implementing long-range visions
Provides opportunities for creativity	Allows for privacy and reflection
Harmonious	Efficient
Quiet	Includes effective and productive people
Has a personal feel to it	
Allows time and space for reflection	Encourages and supports autonomy
Organized	Allows opportunities for creativity
	Task-focused

INFP	**INTP**
Attracts pleasant and committed people focused on values of importance to others	Attracts independent thinkers focused on solving complex problems
Cooperative atmosphere	Allows for privacy
Allows privacy	Fosters independence
Flexible	Flexible
Unbureaucratic	Quiet
Calm and quiet	Unstructured
Allows time and space for reflection	Rewards self-determination

Table 9. Preferred Work Environments for Each Type (continued)

ENFP	ENTP
Attracts imaginative people focused on human possibilities	Attracts independent people working on models to solve complex problems
Colorful	Flexible
Participative atmosphere	Change-oriented
Offers variety and challenge	Includes competent people
Idea-oriented	Rewards risk-taking
Unconstrained	Encourages autonomy
Lively	Unbureaucratic

ENFJ	ENTJ
Attracts individuals focused on changing things for the betterment of others	Attracts results-oriented, independent people focused on solving complex problems
People-oriented	Goal-oriented
Supportive and social	Efficient systems and people
Has a spirit of harmony	Challenging
Encourages expression of self	Rewards decisiveness
Settled	Includes tough-minded people
Orderly	Structured

From *Introduction to Type in Organizations* (2nd ed.) by S. K. Hirsh and J. M. Kummerow, 1990, Palo Alto, CA: Consulting Psychologists Press. Copyright 1990 by Consulting Psychologists Press. Reprinted by permission.

Others find a particular work environment which still allows them to use favorite job activities. For example, an accountant (with any MBTI preference) high on Conventional and Artistic themes may end up working in the finance department of an arts organization.

Finally, it may be that the particular job can be molded to fit personality and interest patterns. An ISTJ receptionist with a C-theme was quite good at keeping track of the details of a busy office, yet needed some breathing space from answering the telephone and time to concentrate on some of her other duties. She arranged to be relieved from her receptionist duties for two hours a day to gain some balance (through Introverted time) in her work. The INFP attorney with a combination Artistic/Social theme switched law firms to find colleagues with whom he feels more compatible and where a more flexible work schedule exists.

Table 10. Work Settings and Holland Codes

Realistic	Investigative
Mechanical	Unstructured
Structured	Flexible
Outdoors where possible	Gadget/book-filled
Working with tools producing tangible products	Intellectual
	Task-oriented
Regular hours	Project-oriented
Clear and unambiguous chain of command	Minimal interaction with chain of command

Artistic	Social
Colorful	Team-oriented
Flexible	Verbally interactive
Unstructured	Flexible
Unpredictable and constantly changing	Warm
"Nothing quite finished"	Group projects
Independent of chain of command	Shared or rotating chain of command

Enterprising	Conventional
Entrepreneurial	Organized
Structured	Well-documented
Expensive	Precise
Impressive	Definite chain of command
Competitive	Tasks clearly defined and documented
Opportunity to impact or assume command	"A place for everything and everything in its place"

Final Comments

The career development process is an ongoing one. All jobs change in one way or another, and finding the right job once will likely not last a lifetime. Clients need to be prepared for recycling through the process many times. As they recycle through the various steps, they are likely to learn more about themselves each time. They may ask about retaking these instruments. Once clients are clear about their MBTI type preferences, they do not need to take it again to see if they have changed, since the MBTI does not measure such change. (They may, however, want to take the *Type Differentiation Indicator,* based on Form J of the MBTI, or the *Expanded Analysis Report,* based on Form K of the MBTI, to give them some information about how they use their type.) Your clients' life experiences may have helped them develop more facility in using specific preferences, although their innate preferences still feel most natural. You may encourage clients to keep their type in mind as they look at their style and to be aware that some activities may come more easily to them than others, based on their personality type.

By contrast, the *Strong* may be retaken and may actually show some differences in clients' vocational pattern as they have been exposed to different careers. However, the research indicates that beyond the age of 25, interest patterns tend to be fairly stable.

These instruments are only tools to help guide people and cannot provide definitive answers. There is much more to us than what these two instruments reveal, but they can be useful guidelines both in helping clients understand their own process of career counseling and in helping them find a more specific direction and career.

References

Brew, S. (1987). *Career development guide for use with the Strong Interest Inventory.* Palo Alto, CA: Consulting Psychologists Press.

Dillon, M., & Weissman, S. (1987, July). Relationship between personality types on the Strong-Campbell and Myers-Briggs instruments. *Measurement and Evaluation in Counseling and Development, 20,* 68–79.

Gottfredson, G. C., Holland, J. L., & Ogawa, D. K. (1982). *Dictionary of Holland occupational codes.* Palo Alto, CA: Consulting Psychologists Press.

Hansen, J. C. (1987). *Strong-Hansen occupational guide.* Palo Alto, CA: Consulting Psychologists Press.

Hansen, J. C., & Campbell, D. P. (1985). *Manual for the Strong Interest Inventory.* Stanford, CA: Stanford University Press.

Hansen, J. C. (1984). *User's guide for the Strong*. Palo Alto, CA: Consulting Psychologists Press.

Hirsh, S. K., & Kummerow, J. M. (1990). *Introduction to type in organizations* (2nd ed.). Palo Alto, CA: Consulting Psychologists Press.

Hirsh, S., & Kummerow, J. (1989). *LIFETypes*. New York: Warner Books.

Hirsh, S. K., & Vessey, T. (1987). *Introduction to the Strong in organizational settings*. Palo Alto, CA: Consulting Psychologists Press.

Kummerow, J. (1987). *Verifying your type preferences: Worksheet and leader's guide*. Gainesville, FL: Center for the Applications of Psychological Type.

Levin, A. (1991). *Introduction to the Strong for career counselors*. Palo Alto, CA: Consulting Psychologists Press.

Macdaid, G. P., McCaulley, M. H., & Kainz, R. I. (1986, 1991). *Atlas of type tables*. Gainesville, FL: Center for the Applications of Psychological Type.

Myers, I. B. (1980, 1990). *Gifts differing*. Palo Alto, CA: Consulting Psychologists Press.

Myers, I. B. (1987). *Introduction to type*. Palo Alto, CA: Consulting Psychologists Press.

Myers, I. B., & McCaulley, M. H. (1985). *Manual: A guide to the development and use of the Myers-Briggs Type Indicator*. Palo Alto, CA: Consulting Psychologists Press.

Nelson, T. L. (1986). *A multivariate analysis of Myers-Briggs personality types in terms of vocational interests*. Unpublished doctoral dissertation, University of Minnesota, Minneapolis–St. Paul.

U.S. Department of Labor. (1977). *Dictionary of occupational titles*. Washington, DC: U.S. Government Printing Office.

U.S. Department of Labor. (1987). *Dictionary of occupational titles* (4th ed. supplement). Washington, DC: U.S. Government Printing Office.

4

· · · · · · · · ·

Competency Profiling:
A New Model for Career Counselors

RICHARD J. MIRABILE

Introduction

Understanding the relationships between people and jobs and the resulting influence such relationships have on performance and satisfaction are of both practical and theoretical importance. From the pragmatic point of view, understanding these relationships could contribute to organizational success vis-à-vis motivation, productivity, turnover, and related areas of institutional life. Theoretically, such information contributes to our general understanding of human behavior and, therefore, adds to the base of knowledge concerning why humans do what they do. However, whether the interest lies in expanding practical or theoretical frameworks, it is essential to ask the right kinds of questions to benefit from the information.

Several important questions that need to be addressed in this regard are the following:

▶ Do people whose knowledge, skills, and ability (KSA or competency) levels match the knowledge, skills, and ability requirements of jobs experience greater or lesser degrees of job satisfaction than individuals whose KSA or competency levels do not match the KSA or competency requirements of jobs?

▶ What is the relationship between high and low levels of job-person match and success on the job?

▶ What are the implications of such information for career counselors and improving client interactions?

The Career Counseling Process

There are multiple sets of functions and activities that career counselors perform. Among them, assisting individuals in the decision-making process relative to career direction seems foremost. This broad area of exploration requires that the counselor learn as much as possible about the client. In that regard, it is common for counselors to administer tests, exploratory questionnaires, values and interests inventories, and a variety of other information gathering tools. These are generally useful and often necessary components of the career counseling process.

In addition to the structured tools and instruments used by many counselors, a significant amount of counseling time is spent in dialogue and direct interaction with the client to help construct the most accurate picture possible relative to his or her career concerns. If one were to describe the process and focus of career counseling, it might look like this:

First, career counseling should always be conducted by professionally trained or certified career counselors. Second, career counseling generally occurs once or several times in a person's career. Third, the focus of career counseling is usually on the following:

▶ Patterns of career satisfaction and dissatisfaction

▶ Broad-based occupational interests

▶ Work/personal/interpersonal values

▶ Competency development

▶ Managerial/supervisory competencies

▶ Administrative competencies

▶ Technical/functional competencies

▶ Life priorities

▶ Family issues and priorities

▶ Leisure activities and interests

▶ Spiritual concerns

▶ Short- and long-term goals

There are two ultimate goals of career counseling activities. First, it is to teach a process—the career exploration and decision-making process. By teaching this process, the counselor empowers the client to continually reassess and reevaluate his or her own situation relative to goals, ambitions, and constantly changing circumstances. This is not to suggest that clients should become their own career counselors; it is rather to suggest that clients can play a more central role in their own career development through knowledge of the career exploration and decision-making process.

Second, an additional goal of career counseling is to establish direction for the client. I do not believe that the goal of the career counseling process is to find a job. There are search firms and employment agencies that fulfill that role quite satisfactorily. Rather, I believe that assisting clients in clarifying a direction in their life is of central importance, for only then can more specific decisions and exploratory activities become meaningful.

This twofold purpose embodies many components, such as empowering clients to take charge of their lives and giving them the skills and tools to conduct a search, write a résumé, take a job interview, and ask the kinds of questions that lead to more career satisfaction in their own lives. However, if one were to cluster the many outcomes of career counseling, I believe that teaching a process and establishing direction are the two primary ones.

Definition of Terms

Numerous terms used in this chapter require additional clarity with respect to definition.

▶ *Job-person congruence*—The degree to which jobs and people match on specified types of variables such as interest, personality, job size, supervisory style, knowledge and skills, organizational structure, and so forth

▶ *Knowledge, skills, and abilities (KSA's)*—Knowledge represents a body of information in a specified area or field (e.g., engineering, marketing, accounting, etc.). Skills, for purposes of this discussion, represent capabilities that may be learned or taught (e.g., communication, delegation, problem solving, etc.). Abilities represent more inherent capabilities or latent talent, such as forms of creativity, general intelligence, or physical dexterity.

▶ *Competencies*—Used interchangeably with KSA's, but also includes such variables as attitudes, traits, and characteristics (e.g., trust, loyalty, or tenacity)

▶ *Job or work environment*—Represents specific characteristics of a work situation such as job type, organization size, pay scale, and working conditions

▶ *Work adjustment*—Observable behaviors such as satisfaction, performance, or job tenure that are a function of the relationship between work personality and work environment

▶ *Work personality*—Characteristics of a person such as age, sex, educational level, or psychological characteristics that comprise variables considered to influence job-person congruence

Assumptions

Several important assumptions underlie this writing. The first is that job-person congruence can be studied vis-à-vis investigating the relationship between the knowledge, skill, and ability (KSA) requirements of jobs and the knowledge, skill, and ability (KSA) levels of individuals. The second assumption is that a positive relationship exists between job-person congruence, reported job satisfaction, and performance levels on the job. Third, it is assumed that this information can be used in a practical application, such as career counseling, to improve those activities in and outside organizations that relate to matching people and jobs.

Competency Profiling and the Job-Person Congruence Connection

At some point in the career counseling process, it is often necessary and appropriate to assist clients in matching their particular career issues with specific occupational environments. This process may be described as *competency profiling*. A working definition of competency profiling is the identification of occupational requirements, an assessment of client competency levels, and a matching process that determines the degree of fit or congruence. In this regard, it behooves counselors to use tools and approaches that facilitate such a goal. Considerable research exists supporting the notion that the more people match the environment in which they work, the more likely they are to experience job satisfaction and to be better performers than those who do not match as well (Schneider, 1985; Wiggins, 1983). There are significant implications in this research because it suggests that counselors might increase their own effectiveness by paying more attention to the job-person congruence connection within the counseling process.

However, it is also important to note that the research in this area has generally relied on matching individuals to work environments using interests, personality characteristics, or organizational variables such as size as the basis of matching (Mirabile, 1988). While these approaches have been successful, the degree of success has not been very great, accounting only for a very small percentage of the difference (5 to 10%) in satisfaction and performance levels between individuals. In simpler terms, this means that other factors account for 90 to 95 percent of the difference in performance and satisfaction levels between individuals. If one examines the career counseling process used by most counselors, it is likely that client interests and personality characteristics are a major point of exploration and discussion. Further, they are often central to the decision-making process itself. This is not to suggest that interests and personality characteristics should not be considered. On the contrary, the intent here is to propose an expanded model that includes perhaps a bit more emphasis on the competency-match idea.

The notion of establishing or identifying client competency levels suggests the need for several types of information. First, assessment methods and instruments need to be created and used to assist in the identification of competency strengths and development areas. Second, assuming counselors were to use this approach, information regarding the competency requirements of specific occupational environments would be a necessary piece of the client-environment matching process. There are several forms of this type of information already in existence. Among the most widely known are the *Dictionary of Occupational Titles* (DOT), the *Occupational Outlook Handbook,* and several computerized programs that contain job information, such as the *System for Interactive Guidance and Information* (SIGI) and the *Education and Career Exploration System* (ECES).

These programs and information represent attempts to provide pro-cesses and tools that facilitate the matching of individuals to specific occupational environments. Here again, however, these sources are generally comprised of information either based on interests and prefer-ences and/or on very general information related to skill sets required in various occupational clusters. The point is not that they are unimportant, it is that newer and more tailored information bases and tools need to be created to facilitate the exploration and decision making of clients with respect to the career counseling process.

For example, imagine as a career counselor that a client wanted to identify his or her relative degree of match or fit with entry-level electrical engineers in an aerospace environment. Assuming that various other career interactions, testing, and explorations were already established, at some point in the process, this type of client would greatly benefit from knowing how well he or she fit this particular environment. In addition, the client would also benefit from knowing the specific competency areas which required additional development to improve the overall degree of fit. To provide this kind of insight to a client, several pieces of information would need to be available. First, it would be necessary to know the specific competency sets required of electrical engineers in general. Second, it would be necessary to know the specific competency sets required of electrical engineers in an aerospace environment. Third, it would be necessary to know the specific competency sets required of entry-level electrical engineers in aerospace as contrasted to middle managers or other levels in a hierarchy.

In addition to knowing the specific competency sets of entry-level engineers in aerospace, however, it is significant to know the different importance or criticality levels of the competencies as well as the proficiency levels required for successful performance in that particular environment. While it is one thing to know which competency sets are required, it is far more useful to know the relative importance each one has to the job or environment as well as the degree to which each one needs to be mastered. In this example, importance or criticality means that if one had a list of 20 competencies that represented successful performance in an entry-level electrical engineering position, it would be extremely useful to know which ones were the most important versus those that were less important relative to each other. Second, one would need to know how proficiently a particular competency would need to be developed for successful performance in an entry-level electrical engineering position or environment.

Here's a simple illustration. Imagine you were making a special salad that required a particular spice to perfect it. This particular spice, then, becomes critical. However, one might only need a pinch of it to complete the salad. Thus, while the spice is important, it is only needed in just a small amount to accomplish the task. Turning to the world of work, while understanding the basics of software programming may be critical for software engineering managers to perform their job successfully, they usually do not have to do the complex programming required of programmers. Software programming is a critical competency for managers, but they do not need to be so proficient at programming that they can actually create programs or teach other people how to program. Likewise, in my job as a consultant, while it is essential that I understand research and statistics (importance) to do my job, I do not have to be a statistician to be successful (proficiency). Thus, the difference between how important or critical a competency is and how proficient one needs to be in applying it is apparent.

In the career counseling process, while counselors seldom have such information available to them, I'm suggesting that acquiring or having access to this type of data could greatly contribute to the person-environment matching component of career decision making. More will be said about how to acquire this information later. For now, the point needs to be stressed that one way to enhance the effectiveness of the career counseling process may lie in spending more time on the matching of clients to specific occupational environments.

What Research Says About Congruence

Many research studies that have focused on job-person interactions have used Holland's (1973) theory of careers as the point of departure. A basic tenet of this theory states that vocational stability, satisfaction, and achievement depend on the congruence between one's personality and the environment in which one works, where congruence is defined as the degree of match or fit between a person and the environment. One corollary of this tenet is that positive vocational choice occurs when individuals are placed, or place themselves, in situations that encourage, reinforce, and reward their distinctive patterns of attitudes, competencies, and interests (Holland, 1973). Numerous studies support Holland's premise that job satisfaction is a function of job-person congruence (Mount & Muchinsky, 1978; Smart, Elton, & McLaughlin, 1978; Spokane, 1985). However, little or no attention has been given to the investigation of job-person congruence using knowledge, skill, and ability requirements of jobs and knowledge, skill, and ability levels of individuals (Schneider, 1985). As we shall see, this is a potentially fruitful area of focus for career counseling. A summary of the most important and relevant research in the area of job-person congruence follows.

Achievement, Stability, Satisfaction, and Congruence Studies. Using a large sample, Rand (1987) examined the relationship between congruence and satisfaction among 7,257 college students from 28 colleges. The results showed a positive relationship between satisfaction and congruence. In a similar study, Morrow (1986) studied samples of math and social science students. Satisfaction with major choice was significantly related to congruence in the math sample only. Nafziger, Holland, and Gottfredson (1983) also found that congruence was related to satisfaction with college in general.

Frantz and Walsh (1972) studied graduate students and found that congruence and consistency (of major choice), when combined, predicted satisfaction and achievement in graduate school whereas congruence and/ or consistency taken alone did not.

More recently, Elton and Rose (1981) used ACT inventory scores and precollege majors to calculate congruence in 2,943 freshmen. They found that congruence was a factor of, but by no means the most important predictor of, dropouts. A final study in this area (Healy & Mourton, 1983) found no significant relationship between congruence and career maturity among community college students.

Findings in Work Environments. Mount and Muchinsky (1978) classified 362 subjects in various occupational groups according to Holland's
topology and then related these classifications to job satisfaction using the
Job Descriptive Indices (JDI). The result was a significantly positive relationship between job satisfaction and congruence in the jobs. In a related
study, Wiggins (1983) used the *Strong Vocational Interest Blanks®* to
measure interest-job congruence. Satisfaction with work and with supervision was related to congruence in workers with long tenure, but not in
those with short tenure.

Personal Adjustment and Congruence. A series of studies by Walsh
and his colleagues examined differences between congruent and incon-
gruent college students on measures of personal adjustment (Walsh &
Russell, 1969), personality (Spokane & Derby, 1979; Walsh & Lewis, 1972),
and self-concept (Leonard, Walsh, & Osipow, 1973). Of the 10 studies
conducted by Walsh and associates, three produced mostly positive results
(Leonard, Walsh, & Osipow, 1973; Walsh & Russell, 1968), two produced
mostly negative results (Walsh, Howard, O'Brien, Santa-Maria, & Edmundson,
1973), and six produced a mixture of positive and negative results
(Spokane & Derby, 1979; Walsh & Lewis, 1972).

Literature Review Summary. The literature reviewed in the area of
job-person congruence reveals several important findings. First, it seems
fairly well established that the relationship, or lack of it, between work
personality and work environment is at minimum a major factor in
explaining job satisfaction, performance, and tenure on the job (Holland,
1973). Second, there is substantial evidence to support the contention
that the greater the degree of job-person match, the greater the level of
reported job satisfaction and the greater the level of performance (Lawler,
1987). Third, virtually all of the research conducted in the area of job-
person congruence has used either personality, interest, or demographic
variables such as age or education level as the descriptors of the person,
and organizational structure, supervisory style, working conditions, and
job content as the environment descriptors (O'Reilly, 1977). Thus, there has
been no investigation of congruence from the perspective of job competency requirements and person competency levels.

What Is a Job Competency?

While research and theory are important elements of building a knowledge
base of information, the translation into useful tools and frameworks is of
equal importance to practitioners. The first step in moving from the realm

of the theoretical to the practical is to identify the most useful definition of the subject matter.

Assuming counselors were to use and/or expand the counseling process to incorporate more emphasis on competency matching, questions arise concerning how to define a competency and which ones to use in client interaction. Various definitions of competence exist. Among them, Klemp (1979) states that a competency is any personal characteristic or attribute that contributes to effective performance and that a job competency is any attribute that contributes to doing a job well. He goes on to say that an attribute can take many forms—it can be a specialized knowledge, an ability, an interest, a trait, a motive, even a self-concept, but that the only way an attribute can become a competency is in its relationship to performance. Therefore, despite the fact that people possess a wide assortment of knowledge, abilities, interests, traits, and motives, unless these attributes contribute to performing a job well, they are not job competencies.

Matching Client Competencies to Job Competencies

Facilitating the counseling process as described above requires the development and use of job-person or job-environment matching processes. There are numerous ways this could be accomplished, from the very simplistic to the very rigorous. The advantage of the simplistic approach is that it provides a quick and easy method for identifying the degree of fit. The disadvantage is that the accuracy or validity of such an approach is questionable at best. The advantage of the rigorous method is that it should provide a fairly high degree of validity. The obvious disadvantage is that these approaches are often cumbersome and time consuming. It would seem to make sense that some combination of the two methods could strike a necessary balance for both counselors and clients.

One way to implement this solution is to move toward automation as the method of assessment and matching. Assume for a minute that information regarding job or work environment competencies was available. If this information could be translated into a form that was useable with a computerized format, then the assessment and matching of client competencies to job or work environment competencies would be extremely quick and likely have a degree of accuracy that would be acceptable for purposes of career counseling. Short of using computers, paper-and-pencil instruments could be used that would provide essentially the same results, but would require additional processing and/or scoring (see Appendix A).

Table 1. Future Marketing Profile

Success Factors

1. Product positioning
2. Coaching
3. Market research
4. Customer satisfaction
5. Contingency planning
6. Change management
7. Sales strategy
8. Competitor analysis
9. Product knowledge
10. Self-development

As for establishing job or work environment competencies, while such data is not easy to come by, it does in fact exist. For example, in my own research, competency profiles have been identified in over a dozen industries representing almost all levels of worker, from clerical to executive. Furthermore, these profiles have been constructed to include the competency, its behavioral definition, an importance ranking for a specific level and industry, as well as the proficiency level required. In some cases, profiles have even been constructed that represent projected future requirements for specific occupational requirements (see Table 1). The point is threefold: first, that the kind of information being suggested in this chapter can be identified; second, that simple or rigorous procedures requiring assessment and matching can also be developed, with particular attention paid to the use of computers; and third, that this type of process, if used by career counselors in conjunction with all the other mechanisms and procedures they currently use, should result in a higher success rate for client outcomes.

The Competency Profiling Model for Career Counselors

In order to add some clarity for counselors to see the flow of activities in the proposed competency profiling model, the following steps represent a comprehensive breakdown of an ideal sequence of steps in the process:

1. Counselor and client agree that specific job or work environment exploration would be useful at a particular point in the counseling process.

2. If possible, they narrow the focus to specific industries or occupational environments.

3. Counselor provides a list of competencies required in whatever industry/job/work environment being explored. (These should be presented in some random or perhaps alphabetical order to eliminate prior knowledge of competency importance.)

4. Client does a self-assessment, either in a computerized version or paper-and-pencil instrument form. In this assessment, they are rating their own competency strengths using a rating scale devised for this type of assessment.

5. If possible, client and counselor obtain additional assessments of the client's relative competency strengths and development areas. Possible raters to include would be current or previous supervisors, peers, subordinates, or anyone familiar with the client's performance relative to the competency list.

6. After the client and others have provided ratings of the client's competency strengths and development areas, the ratings can be averaged to arrive at a composite picture of the client.

7. This "profile" of the client can then be compared to the specific job or work environment competencies to determine the relative degree of fit. Figure 1 shows a computerized version of this matching process comparing a client's self-assessment on a set of sales competencies to an established profile for sales manager in a high-tech environment. On the scale of 1 to 5, 1 = low, 3 moderate, and 5 = advanced level of proficiency.

8. The difference between client competency strengths and required competency levels, assuming acceptance by counselor and client as reasonably accurate, could then be used to establish development plans that address the gaps (see Figure 2).

While this is clearly an abbreviated version of the actual flow of activities, and while it assumes access to particular types of information regarding competency requirements, it does illustrate the point. The process described could easily be repeated for other types of jobs in the same or other industries, providing clients and counselors with valuable information regarding job-environment match. Coupled with information from tests, inventories, and general exploration sessions, it seems that the ability of counselors to enhance the counseling outcome would be considerably enhanced.

Figure 1. Proficiency Comparison for Jane Andrews

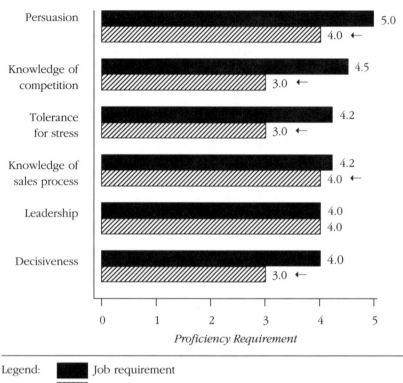

Legend:
- Job requirement
- Client profile
- ← Develop to improve fit

Gathering the Competency Information

Assuming the value of using a competency match process is seen, it begs the question of how to gather such information concerning job or industry requirements. Here are a few possibilities. First, through professional organizations that support the counseling profession, it might be possible to organize an effort to research and identify competency data. Second, it might also be possible to write a grant demonstrating the potential effectiveness of adding a competency model to the counseling process. Third, university counseling centers might be able to gather competency data through their contacts with business and industry groups. Fourth, a special task force could be set up consisting of academicians, counselors, business and industry experts, and others, joined together for the expressed purpose of identifying a core set of competency data across industries. Fifth, counselors might be able to conduct simple research or inquiries from

Figure 2. Next Steps for Development

Employee: Jane Andrews   Job: Regional Sales Manager

In order to improve the skill level for this objective, the success factors listed below are the ones you should concentrate on. To maximize the development process, we suggest that the developmental focus be on only 2 or 3 factors at a time. The simplest way to decide which factors to select is to first determine how critical the factor is to the objective. The list is in descending order of importance, so *the closer the factor is to the top of the list, the more important it is.* Another consideration is to *pick those employee factors that are the greatest distance from the objective levels.* To do this, simply look at the bar graph and see where the biggest gaps between the objective level and employee level are. This combined with the importance level should give you what you need to choose.

Success Factors to Improve the Fit

Importance Ranking	Success Factor	Job Requirement Level	Employee Proficiency Level
1	Persuasion	5.0	4.0
2	Knowledge of competition	4.5	3.0
3	Tolerance for stress	4.2	3.0
6	Decisiveness	4.0	3.0
9	Multiple focus	3.7	3.0
11	Knowledge of market channel	3.3	2.0

local industries regarding the nature of competency data, perhaps forming a combined counselor-industry council. For example, a task force of business and education leaders in Los Angeles was formed to establish the skill requirements needed in industries for the coming decade in order to translate that information into relevant curriculum. Such a task force will necessarily have to gather the type of competency information discussed in this chapter to fulfill their mission. (See the case study at the end of this chapter.)

The real point is whether counselors perceive that adding or supplementing what they do with a competency match process would be beneficial. If yes, then an effort needs to be mobilized to create such a system, with counselors identifying the roles they would play in that scenario.

A Note on Standardized Ability Tests. While standardized ability tests already exist, the competency profiling approach uses specific sets of competencies drawn from specific organizations or occupational environments. Further, the process includes establishing the relative importance and proficiency requirement for each competency in each job classification. Thus, the resulting profile is highly tailored versus generic. While standardized ability tests can be quite useful, they use bases of comparison (norms) that may not be relevant to a specific job target within a specific industry.

Conclusions

The purpose of this chapter has been to explore and present the idea of supplementing or improving the work career counselors do with the use of a person-environment matching process. The intention of such a model is to suggest one method of enhancing the relative effectiveness of the career counseling outcome. It is not to suggest that other methods and exploratory procedures traditionally used by career counselors should be abandoned or that they are not useful. Further, it proposes that in examining the intended purpose of a career counseling intervention, we can determine whether a competency-based, person-environment matching process would be beneficial. This rationale is based on solid research evidence which indicates that the greater the match between person competency levels and job competency requirements, the greater the success (performance) and satisfaction on the job. Clearly, significant work needs to be done to operationalize such a system, but the possibilities for expanding the power and effectiveness of the counseling process are exciting.

As professionals dedicated to helping others explore the possibilities in their own lives, it behooves counselors themselves to explore possibilities that lie within their reach. Only then will we shape the future of the profession and expand the vision of effective helping professionals.

References

Elton, C. F., & Rose, H. A. (1981). *Retention revisited: With congruence, differentiation and consistency.* Unpublished manuscript, University of Kentucky, Lexington.

Frantz, T. T., & Walsh, E. P. (1972). Exploration of Holland's theory of vocational choice in graduate school environments. *Journal of Vocational Behavior, 2,* 223–232.

Healy, C. C., & Mourton, D. L. (1983). Derivations of the self-directed search: Potential clinical and evaluative uses. *Journal of Vocational Behavior, 23,* 318–328.

Holland, J. L. (1973). *Making vocational choices* (1st ed.). Englewood Cliffs, NJ: Prentice-Hall.

Klemp, G. (1979). Job competence assessment. *Training and Development Journal, 26,* 72–81.

Lawler, E. E. (1987). *Motivation in work organizations.* Monterey, CA: Brooks/Cole.

Leonard, R. L., Walsh, W. B., & Osipow, S. H. (1973). Self-esteem, self-consistency, and second vocational choice. *Journal of Counseling Psychology, 20,* 91-93.

Mirabile, R. (1988). *Job-person congruence, performance and satisfaction.* Unpublished doctoral dissertation, The Fielding Institute, Santa Barbara, CA.

Morrow, J. M., Jr. (1986). A test of Holland's theory. *Journal of Counseling Psychology, 18,* 422–425.

Mount, M. K., & Muchinsky, P. M. (1978). Person-environment congruence and employee job satisfaction: A test of Holland's theory. *Journal of Vocational Behavior, 13,* 84–100.

Nafziger, D. H., Holland, J. L., & Gottfredson, G. D. (1983). Student-college congruency as a predictor of satisfaction. *Journal of Counseling Psychology, 22,* 132–139.

O'Reilly, C. (1977). Personality-job fit: Implications for individual attitudes and performance. *Organizational Behavior and Human Performance, 18,* 36–46.

Schneider, B. (1985). *The people make the place.* Presidential address to the Society for Industrial and Organizational Psychology, American Psychological Association, Los Angeles.

Smart, J., Elton, C., & McLaughlin, G. (1978). Person-environment congruence and job satisfaction. *Journal of Vocational Behavior, 29,* 216–225.

Spokane, A. R. (1985). A review of research on person-environment congruence in Holland's theory of careers. *Journal of Vocational Behavior, 26,* 306–343.

Spokane, A. R., & Derby, D. P. (1979). Locus of control, ego strength, and congruence in college women. *Journal of Vocational Behavior, 15,* 36–42.

Walsh, W. B., & Lewis, R. O. (1972). Consistent, inconsistent, and undecided career preferences and personality. *Journal of Vocational Behavior, 2,* 309–316.

Walsh, W. B., & Russell, J. H. (1969). College major choice and personal adjustment. *Personnel and Guidance Journal, 47,* 685–688.

Wiggins, J. D. (1983). The relation of job satisfaction to vocational preferences among teachers of the educatable mentally retarded. *Journal of Vocational Behavior, 8,* 13–18.

Case Study

A large insurance company needed an analysis of the training and development needs for the supervisors and managers of the company's data processing division. The company wanted to accomplish two goals. The first was to identify the overall training needs of the data processing supervisors and managers and to determine what specific training needs should be given the highest priority. The second goal was to develop specific training plans for each individual and begin to identify career paths for individual supervisors and managers. Of particular interest was the determination of which supervisors had the skills and abilities necessary for promotion to the job of manager. In order to meet these goals, the organization needed to develop processes for (a) identifying the critical competencies for both the supervisor and manager job, (b) determining the difference between the jobs in terms of the competencies each required, and (c) measuring each individual's mastery of the important competencies.

Project Design

In brief, the project design consisted of three major parts. The first involved identifying the competencies necessary for successful performance in both the manager's and supervisor's position. The second involved the development of procedures for measuring the individual job incumbent's mastery of these competencies. The third involved the use of the information generated to assess specific training and development needs.

Part 1: Identifying Competency Requirements

Before training needs can be directly assessed, a thorough understanding of job requirements is necessary. The objective of the first part of the study was to develop as complete an understanding as possible of the knowledge and skill sets required to successfully perform in each of the positions. To identify the requirements for the supervisor and manager jobs, the following procedures were used.

Step One: A series of structured job analysis interviews were conducted with a set of job incumbents and their supervisors. These interviews focused on the major tasks, responsibilities, knowledge and skill requirements of the job, time spent in various activities, and perceptions of other factors related to successful job performance. Following this, a thorough analysis of the interview data was conducted and the information translated into statements reflecting behaviorally anchored job competencies. Each job competency represented a separate knowledge, skill, or ability (KSA)

Table 2. Sample List of Job Competencies

Analytical Thinking

Discriminates between important and unimportant details, recognizes inconsistencies between facts, and draws correct inferences from information

Forecasting

Accurately anticipates changes in workloads, resources, personnel needs, etc., as a result of changes in the work situation, technology, or external developments

Goal-orientation

Ensures that the results to be achieved by the division, units, teams, or individuals are clearly defined and understood at all times

Knowledge of Subordinate Jobs

Has a thorough understanding of the purpose, general tasks, and knowledge and skill requirements of the jobs under one's supervision

Knowledge of User Support Areas

Has a basic understanding of the various user areas being supported and of their needs and technical requirements

Multiple Focus

Effectively manages a large number (i.e., 10 to 15) of different and often conflicting objectives, projects, groups, or activities at one time

Organizational Knowledge

Has a thorough understanding of organizational policies, procedures, and key personnel, which enables a manager/supervisor to effectively carry out job responsibilities

Priority Setting

Identifies and separates those tasks that are most important from those that are less important; maintains a clear sense of priorities and a vision of the larger picture

Risk Taking

Takes risks when the consequences are difficult to predict but the payoffs are likely to be great, even when proposals may be rejected by supervisors or when one's image may suffer if wrong

---

identified as necessary for high performance. The first draft of the competency statements was shown to a sample of job incumbents who were instructed to edit, revise, and, most importantly, to make sure that the list did not omit any competency necessary for the performance of their jobs. Based on their comments and suggestions, a final list of competency statements was developed. A sample of the final list of 72 competencies is shown in Table 2.

Step Two: The final list of competency statements represented all the separate knowledge, skills, and abilities necessary to perform either the manager or supervisor job. The second step in the project involved describing each job using the set of competency items. To do this, each manager and supervisor was given the complete set of competency statements and instructed in how to profile his or her job. The profiling process consisted of categorizing the competency statements in terms of how important each was for successful performance in the specific position the individual held, either "manager" or "supervisor." All responses from these supervisors and managers were used to create consensus profiles for those respective positions.

Step Three: Although the profiles describe the relative importance of each competency for successful job performance, they do not completely specify the level of the competency required for high performance. Some competencies, even though important for the job, may not require detailed understanding or an advanced level of mastery. Other competencies, although of less importance for job performance, may demand a higher level of mastery. To determine the level at which each competency must be mastered, a set of senior managers rated the proficiency levels required of each competency, and based upon their answers, overall proficiency levels were determined for the important competencies of both jobs.

Once these three steps were completed, both the supervisor and manager jobs could be described as a profile of the specific competencies necessary for effective performance and the level at which each competency must be mastered.

Part 2: Using the Competency Information

Once the competency information and job profiles were created, they could then be used in a variety of ways within the organization. In this particular example, the insurance company used the competency information to evaluate specific individuals against the competency data to determine training and development needs. The way they did this was as follows.

First, they asked each individual to rate him or herself against each of the competencies using a simple scale of one to five where one represented minimal competency, three represented moderate competency, and five represented maximum competency development. Next, they asked each employee's manager or supervisor to also assess the employee using the same scale. Finally, the employee and the manager each selected two peers to evaluate the employee on each competency.

The results of all ratings were averaged together to derive a profile of the employee. This profile was then compared or matched to the job profile that was created. The outcome of this matching process was a fairly clear picture of the development gaps that existed for each employee relative to each competency. (A development gap is the difference between a job competency requirement and a person competency level, where the job competency requirement is greater than the person competency level. For example, if the job competency requirement for problem-solving skills was rated five and the person competency rating was four, this would be considered a developmental gap.)

The job-person matching process was done for all employees in the department. The results yielded not only individual pictures of each employee's strengths and weaknesses, but it also identified the most critical training needs of the entire department. From that point, it was relatively simple to determine exactly where the training and development efforts should be focused and who should be developed in exactly which areas. This is precisely what the insurance company did and continues to do presently.

Appendix A: Critical Competency Assessment

The following worksheet has been designed to assist in the evaluation of key competency areas for (here you would list the job or work competency areas such as engineering, marketing, etc.). These particular competencies are considered important for successful performance. The worksheet will be used by both clients as well as by other sets of raters so two sets of instructions have been included. Please read the instructions that apply to you.

Instructions for Clients

Please read the following list of competencies carefully and then evaluate yourself on each using the Proficiency Levels rating sheet that has been provided. Do not try to compare yourself against other people, simply circle the number that most closely reflects your current level of proficiency for each competency as you believe it to be. In all cases, use the column marked C (Client). In addition, whenever you estimate your proficiency level to be a 4 or 5, try to provide some relevant and concrete evidence of your estimate.

Instructions for Other Raters

Please read the following list of competencies carefully, and then evaluate this individual on each one, using the Proficiency Levels rating sheet that has been provided. Do not attempt to compare this person against anyone else. Simply circle the number that most closely reflects your best estimate of his or her proficiency level for each competency. In all cases, use the column marked O (Other). In addition, a comment section has been included so that you may respond to a particular category or evidence statement. It is only necessary to comment when your rating differs from this individual's rating.

Leadership Skills	C	O
Effectively works through others in order to accomplish	0	0
objectives; builds cooperative relationships; sees the	1	1
long-range implications of issues/decisions and develops	2	2
short- and long-term solutions; wins the respect, trust,	3	3
and confidence of others.	4	4
	5	5

Evidence:

Supervisor Comment:

Proficiency Levels

Level 0: Not Applicable/Observable

Use a "0" rating to indicate that the factor either does not apply or that it has not been observed adequately to assess.

Level 1: Minimal Knowledge/Development

This level reflects only a talking knowledge, a general familiarity of terms, or a low level of the skill/ability. Close supervision is required at this level in order to apply it.

Level 3: Moderate Knowledge/Development

This level reflects a working knowledge or the skill or ability to apply it without close supervision.

Level 5: Advanced Knowledge/Development

This level reflects comprehensive knowledge or a high degree of skill/ ability. At this level, one has mastered the specific knowledge, skill, or ability to the extent that instruction of others in its application is possible.

II

· · · · · · · · ·

New Directions
in the Workplace

5

• • • • • • • • •

The Realignment of Workers and Work in the 1990s

ANDREA SAVERI

Introduction

The labor force is in the midst of profound structural changes. Demographic trends such as the aging of baby boomers, the "very olding" of a large segment of the population, and the shrinking portion of youth will have their full impact on the labor force in the 1990s. Immigration and high growth rates in nonwhite populations will continue to transform the population and result in increasing ethnic diversity. In addition, the number of men and women in the labor force will almost be equal for the first time. Women's participation rates have climbed steadily since 1970 and now are close to those of men.

Intense global competition, restructuring of domestic corporations, and consolidation of companies worldwide through mergers and acquisitions are some of the key driving forces that will continue to transform employment during the 1990s. Not only will workers be employed in different kinds of jobs in the future, but the nature of work itself will change.

Organizations that use information as a raw material will flourish in the 1990s. More workers will find employment in service-producing industries and in information-based jobs indirectly related to the production of goods. At the same time, however, manufacturing will contribute 34 percent to the total dollar output generated by industries in 2000. Fewer workers actually will produce goods. Rather, they will orchestrate the production of goods through automation and other uses of technology. As Peter Drucker describes the information-based organization of the 1990s,[*] both management and nonmanagement level workers will need to be able to search and retrieve data and apply specialized knowledge to develop information relevant to the organization's operation. The widespread use of information technology and telecommunications will enable managers to lead their employees in new ways. Employees will be expected to engage in more cooperative work and make key operational decisions on the job because of their heightened access to information via technology. For this reason, workers of the future will be *knowledge workers*.

The challenge for the next decade is to align the new work force with the new workplace. Educators, counselors, and human resource specialists will play a key role in developing the work force of the 1990s so it can function smoothly and effectively in this new world of work. The realignment of the work force not only will affect youths and entry-level workers but older, experienced workers as well. Career counselors, educators, and trainers will be expected to identify the mismatches and gaps between workers and the workplace and to develop strategies to achieve a better fit. In order to do this, career counselors must understand the underlying changes in the work force. That way, they can help their clients plan ahead, develop skills, and set career goals that will be achievable in the new work environment.

The first part of this chapter discusses key growth, age, gender, and ethnic shifts in the work force that will help counselors spot opportunities and challenges for workers planning their careers. The second part of the chapter looks at how occupations are changing from production-based jobs to information-based jobs. It also identifies industries where this change is most prevalent. This will help counselors identify particular industries and occupations that offer job mobility and career growth.

Shifts in the Labor Force in the 1990s

Growth Trend of the Labor Force

The first striking feature about the work force of the 1990s is that it will grow much more slowly than in any other decade since the 1930s. Growth will be the slowest during the first half of the decade, and it will increase to just over 1 percent in the second half, when the echo-boom cohort (those born in the late 1970s) begins to enter the labor market (see Figure 1). As a result, educated young entry-level workers of the early 1990s will be in a good bargaining position. Later in the decade, competition will pick up slightly.

---

[*]Peter Drucker, "The Coming of the New Organization," *Harvard Business Review,* January–February, 1988.

**Figure 1. Average Annual Rate of Change,
in the Civilian Labor Force, 1960–2000**

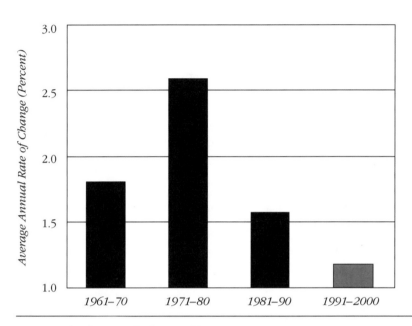

Note: On this figure and others to follow, shaded bar signifies projected data.

Source: IFTF; derived from historical data from the U.S. Bureau of Labor Statistics, labor force statistics derived from the Current Population Survey, 1948–87, Table A–9, Employment and Earnings, January 1990, Table A–3, and *Monthly Labor Review,* November 1989, Table 1.

In contrast, during the 1970s the labor force grew at an average annual rate of 2.6 percent. Roughly 2.4 million workers entered the work force each year, and employers had a large number of applicants from which to choose. In the 1990s, growth will be slower and employers will have to dip deeper into a shrinking labor pool rather than skimming from the top as they have done in past decades. This means that skilled and knowledgeable workers will stand out. Counselors should encourage workers to leverage their skills and experience when planning their careers.

Maturation of the Labor Force

There will be over 141 million workers in the year 2000. This equals a net increase of 15 million workers during the 1990s—the smallest increase since the 1960s (see Table 1). Demographic shifts illustrate the dynamic change within the labor force—change that will bring about new career needs during the 1990s. The changing size of age cohorts shows that the

Table 1. Number of Workers in the Civilian Labor Force Aged 16 Years and Over, 1960–2000

Year	Workers (in millions)
1960	69.6
1970	82.8
1980	106.9
1988	121.7
1990	126.1
2000	**141.1**

Note: On this table and others to follow, bold numbers signify projections for the year 2000.

Source: IFTF; derived from historical data from the U.S. Bureau of Labor Statistics, labor force statistics derived from the Current Population Survey, 1948–87, Table A–9, Employment and Earnings, January 1990, Table A–3, and *Monthly Labor Review*, November 1989, Table 1.

labor force, like the population in general, is aging. By 2000, the average age of a worker will be 39.3 years—significantly older than the current average of 35.9 years.

More workers seeking career advice will be well established; they will have families, with responsibilities to spouses, children, and older parents. Many will have some past work experience. Their financial concerns will be greater than less settled, younger workers. Counselors and other human resource professionals must realize that the expectations of these older workers are different from younger workers. Job security, health benefits, and income will be high priorities for them.

Baby boomers will have a tremendous impact on the labor force in the 1990s for two reasons:

▶ They are a large group. As they mature, they will boost the number of workers older than 35 years.

▶ The participation of women 25 through 44 years old will continue to increase during the 1990s. Female baby boomers will be distinctly different from the same age cohort in previous years. Older and younger baby boom women will have different expectations of their employers and their career choices. Counselors should learn to identify these differences among baby boom women to provide meaningful and practical guidance.

The youngest baby boomer turned 25 years old in 1990 (the oldest turned 45). The much smaller baby-bust cohort (those born between 1965

Figure 2. Growth in the Labor Force—Average Annual Percent Change of Civilian Work Force by Age Cohort, 1991–2000

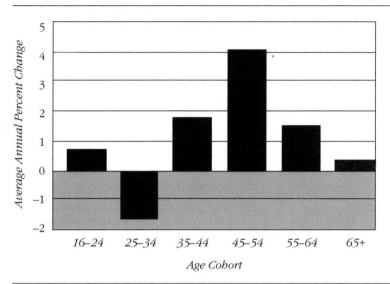

Source: IFTF; derived from historical data from the U.S. Bureau of Labor Statistics, labor force statistics derived from the Current Population Survey, 1948–87, Table A–9, Employment and Earnings, January 1990, Table A–9, and *Monthly Labor Review*, November 1989, Table 4.

and 1975) was between 15 and 25 years old in 1990. Fewer people in this group means much slower growth in the number of high school graduates and new entrants into the labor market. By the year 2000, the baby-bust cohort will be the young workers in the labor force aged 25 through 35. They will make up a much smaller share of the future work force (see Figure 2).

The labor force age-breakdown in 1980 and in 2000 shows the dramatic difference in impact from the baby boom group (see solid bars in Figure 3). The work force age pyramid in 1980 resembles the traditional organizational structure in the workplace and fits neatly with traditional organizational needs. There are many entry-level workers and jobs, fewer middle-level positions, and a small group that directs and manages the organization (see Figure 3). In the year 2000, there will be more older workers who want to move up the organizational ladder, yet fewer positions will be available as organizations reduce their middle-level management work force. A major challenge for employers is to develop new job functions that fit into a horizontal organizational structure. These

**Figure 3. Comparison of the Labor Force Age Breakdown
for 1980 and 2000**

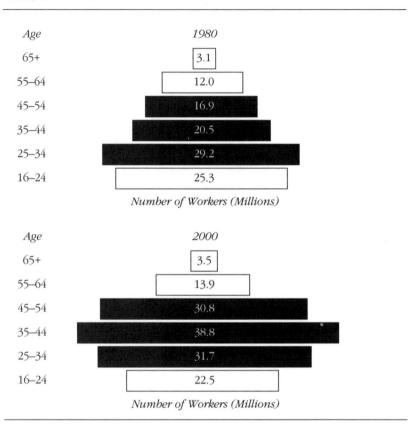

Age	1980
65+	3.1
55–64	12.0
45–54	16.9
35–44	20.5
25–34	29.2
16–24	25.3

Number of Workers (Millions)

Age	2000
65+	3.5
55–64	13.9
45–54	30.8
35–44	38.8
25–34	31.7
16–24	22.5

Number of Workers (Millions)

Source: IFTF; derived from historical data from the U.S. Bureau of Labor Statistics, labor force statistics derived from the Current Population Survey, 1948–87, Table A–9, Employment and Earnings, January 1990, Table A–3, and *Monthly Labor Review*, November 1989, Table 4.

new positions will capture workers who otherwise may fall out of the pyramid. Career counselors should be aware of the organizational changes that either will create or limit career opportunities for middle-aged and older workers. Workers will need assistance leveraging their skills so that they can make smooth transitions into new positions that may not be vertical moves in the organizational structure.

In the year 2000, half the labor force will be between the ages of 35 and 54. Over 70 percent will be between 25 and 54 in 2000, compared to 62 percent in 1980. The following are some of the most important human resource and management-related issues that counselors, educators, and trainers will have to consider as a result of the maturing of the labor force:

▶ *Constant need for retraining.* As jobs become more complex and more information-related, workers will need to be retrained continually in order to maintain their productivity. Training will become an integral part of each worker's job—at both management and nonmanagement levels. Training should be a key point of discussion for counselors and their clients.

▶ *Heightened responsibilities to family.* Care for children and elderly dependents will be a major concern for maturing employees. Balancing work demands with family demands will be a challenge for a large percentage of men and women in the work force. Employers must evaluate strategies to support working members of families, but not all will choose or be able to take action. Counselors will have to work closely with their clients to help them specify their priorities in terms of time, family commitments, and other obligations. Such a priority list will help determine the best career strategy.

▶ *Fewer young workers to fill entry-level jobs.* Employers will need to fill entry-level jobs, and career counselors can play a large role in providing a scarce resource—young workers. Counselors who work with the young should join efforts with local employers looking for entry-level workers. Their cooperation in preparing workers for the workplace will benefit both employers and workers. Young workers will need appropriate training and basic education in order to develop their fullest potential. The use of technology to automate routine tasks will help employers adjust to the smaller entry-level work force.

▶ *Special needs of and uses for older workers.* Almost 18 million workers will be 55 years or older in 2000. Employers may need to devise special programs to capture the experience of these workers and keep them on the job. Part-time or contractual arrangements with benefits may keep older, experienced workers on the job longer. Teaming older workers with younger, entry-level workers may help ease the training burden for employers and boost both the morale and value of older workers. Counselors should educate workers to the demographic changes in the labor force so that they will see the benefits from pairing older and younger workers. Counselors also may include employers on their list of people who need to be educated about the benefits of older employees mentoring younger employees.

▶ *Strategic use of benefits.* Employers will seek strategic uses for
health and other benefits in order to retain and attract workers. In
particular, health benefits for retirees will be a major concern for
employers. Family-related benefits (child and elder care and flexible
work policies) will attract working women (single and married),
working couples, and workers with elderly parents. Counselors
should help workers identify which benefits are most meaningful
and relevant, for example, child care and prenatal benefits for
family members, and how to negotiate for them. Workers' satisfaction with an employer is often higher when benefits are more
flexible and generous.

Women in the Labor Force

The changing pattern of women's participation in the work force will be
a major source of its growth and compositional change in the next decade.
In 2000, women will make up almost half the labor force—up from 38
percent in 1970. Women's participation in the labor force (i.e., the percent
of women who are in the labor force) for every age group has increased
continuously since 1970 (see Figure 4).

Only 43.3 percent of all women participated in the labor force in 1970.
That figure will reach over 62 percent in 2000. The participation rate for
women always has remained below the participation rate for the civilian
labor force as a whole. By the year 2000, however, the gap will close to an
approximate 6 percent difference, compared to a 17 percent difference in
1970. Counselors can gain more insight into the implications of women's
increased participation by comparing key characteristics of two specific
age cohorts for different years.

Several studies report that senior women in the labor force today
(women who entered in the 1970s) are quite different from the younger
women currently entering the work force. The difference is particularly
clear for both senior and junior women in corporate management;
education levels have increased, and attitudes toward marriage, childbearing,
and career have changed. All of these will influence decisions made by
women entering the work force in the 1990s. Understanding the background of younger and older women in the work force will help career
counselors develop strategies to help workers make smooth transitions
throughout their careers.

Women who were 15 to 34 years old in the 1980s will be the women
who make up the 25- to 44-year-old work force cohort of the 1990s.
Looking ahead will help identify the issues that will emerge in the
workplace and will be of primary concern to career counselors. This long-
term look will enable them to inform their clients about steps they can take
today to improve their employability.

**Figure 4. Civilian Labor Force Participation Rates—
Total Labor Force and Women by Age, 1970–2000**

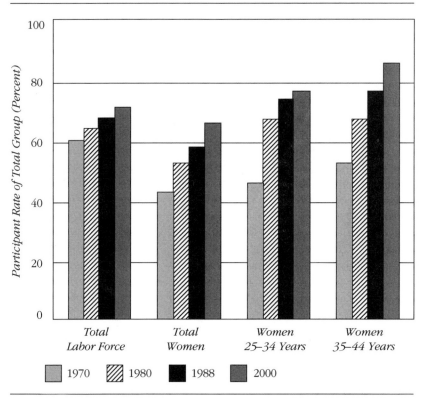

Source: IFTF; drived from labor force statistics. Derived from the Current Population
Survey, 1948–87, Table A-10, and *Monthly Labor Review,* November 1989, Table 4.

Women 15 to 24 Years Old. There were about the same number of young
women aged 15 to 24 in 1987 as in 1970—just over 18 million in the civilian
population. Consequently, as these women age during the 1990s, the
number of entry-level-aged women in the work force will not increase
substantially. However, the share of black, Hispanic, and Asian women in
this age group will increase to almost one third of all women by 2000. Thus,
the 1990s will see an increasing number of nonwhite 15- to 24-year-olds
looking for work. Differences in education level, language, and cultural
values concerning marriage, childbearing, and work outside the home will
influence their participation in the work force for many years to come.

By age 24, most young men and women have entered the labor market
for the first time as full-time workers. Educational attainment for women
20 to 24 years old in a given year indicates the level of educational

**Figure 5. Percent of Women 20 to 24 Years of Age
With 1 to 3 Years of College**

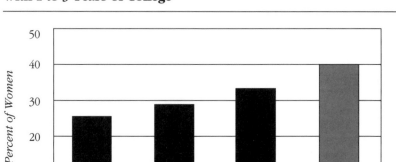

Source: IFTF; derived from historical data from the U. S. Bureau of the Census, Current Population Reports, Series P-20, Nos. 207, 390, and 428, *Educational Attainment in the United States*.

achievement of potential entry-level women workers (see Figure 5). More young women are going to college, graduating, and continuing their education beyond college, while a decreasing proportion of young women complete their education at the high school level. By the year 2000, many of these young women with some college will complete four-year degrees.

Occupational mobility and advancement from entry-level positions will become easier and less restrictive as more women complete higher levels of education. In the 1990s, more women 20 to 24 years old will be prepared to enter the labor force at higher occupational levels and to take on greater supervisory and managerial responsibilities than in the 1970s, when completion levels were lower. Their ability to learn on the job will be enhanced with more years of school behind them. However, employers will need to screen workers and assess training needs carefully because there still will be a sizable portion (about one-third) of women in this age group in 2000 with only a high school diploma or less. Counselors should stress continuous skill improvement as a strategy for young women to stand out in the hiring pool. Employers will look harder for these women.

Women 25 to 34 Years Old. The number of women aged 25 to 34 increased substantially in the 1980s, but it will decrease slightly in the 1990s to about 18 million. Similar to the 15 to 24 year olds, the share of nonwhite women will increase.

At age 25, most women face several career and lifestyle choices that will characterize their participation in the labor force. Among the most critical choices are:

▶ *Family*—to get married or remain single and to have children or postpone childbearing

▶ *Education*—whether to pursue higher levels of education, and whether it should be professional or technical, full or part-time

▶ *Employment*—whether to work in the labor force full or part-time or to leave the labor force

In the 1970s and 1980s, women faced these alternatives and several pioneered new pathways that combined the choices and broke down the traditional roles of women. Their labor force participation increased tremendously in the 1970s—from about 43 percent to 57 percent. They made big gains in college-level attainment. Women 25 to 34 years old initiated dramatic changes in marriage and childbearing patterns. More women decided to postpone getting married or having children, and they gave education and work equal or higher priority at that time in their lives. Women at this age in 1970 (now about 45–55 years old) entered the work force in great numbers, yet they made different trade-offs between work and family than women will make in the 1990s. Many of these older women are reentering the work force today after leaving work to raise their children.

In the 1990s, women will continue to face the same choices as their counterparts did in the 1970s and 1980s. However, the labor force will be affected differently because fewer women will leave work permanently after having a child. Childbearing and labor force participation will be more integrated in the 1990s as it becomes more difficult economically for women to stay at home. This will be particularly true for less educated women, many of them ethnic minorities working in low-skilled service occupations. Census Bureau data have shown that if child care is accessible, labor force participation for women with young children will increase—as much as 20 percent for some subgroups. Those most positively affected by the prospect of accessible child care will be unmarried or never-married women and those with a high school education or less, who have had child care constraints on working.

Education as a Key Factor in Job Mobility for Women. Both the number and percentage of women 25 to 34 years old who completed postsecondary years of education increased sharply between 1970 and 1987 (see Figure 6).

**Figure 6. Women 25 to 34 Years of Age
With 4 or More Years of College**

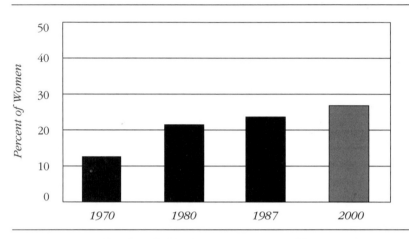

Source: IFTF; derived from historical data from the U. S. Bureau of the Census, Current Population Reports, Series P-20, Nos. 207, 390, and 428, *Educational Attainment in the United States.*

The importance of a higher degree to a person's employability also has grown since the 1970s. Consequently, there have been more women older than the typical college age (18–24 years old) enrolling in college. From 1975 to 1987, the number of women 25 to 34 years old enrolled in college for degree work grew by 50 percent from almost 1 million women to almost 1.5 million women. And the number of college-enrolled women aged 35 and older increased just as rapidly—they numbered 614,000 in 1975 and increased to almost 1.2 million in 1987.

The payoff to these women will be great in the 1990s as more jobs will require advanced degrees, a wider array of skills, and higher skill levels. Counselors should encourage older women to complete higher levels of education if they can manage it. Family and work responsibilities make it prohibitive for many women to go to school or attend training programs after work. One strategy may be to help women find employment where there are opportunities on the job for training and skill upgrading. These are job attributes that counselors should point out to their clients.

While as a whole women aged 25 to 34 years have made gains in completing higher levels of education, a larger share of black and Hispanic women still have significantly less education (see Figure 7). This is a critical issue for counselors during the 1990s, since ethnic women will account for an increasingly larger share of the population and the work force. Counselors should encourage these women to go on to higher levels of

**Figure 7. Educational Attainment of Women
25 to 29 Years of Age by Ethnicity**

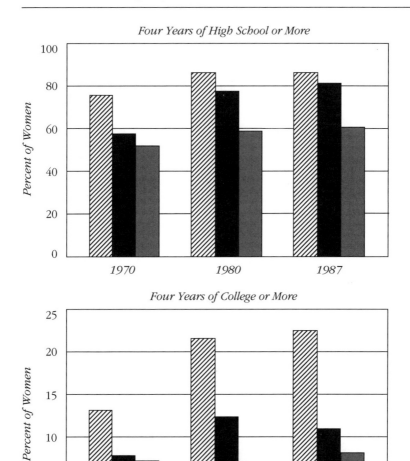

Four Years of High School or More

Four Years of College or More

White   Black   Hispanic

Note: Hispanic data are for 1975; not available for 1970.

Source: IFTF; derived from historical data from the U. S. Bureau of the Census, Current Population Reports, Series P-20, Nos. 207, 390, and 428, *Educational Attainment in the United States*.

education, especially in areas like science and engineering where advanced training is an asset. A higher level of education will be a source of leverage in the job market. Counselors must recognize the diversity among women looking for work. Particular job-hunting strategies may be more appropriate for some women while not that helpful to others. Counselors should work closely with employers to develop more effective recruiting and job preparation strategies that will better match a diverse group of workers with available jobs. Helping ethnic women attain higher levels of education will be a critical and strategic issue for educators and corporate trainers in the 1990s, as ethnic women increase in number and as their rate of participation in the work force approaches the level of white women.

Marriage Trends for Women. Marriage patterns for women have been changing since 1970, when a larger proportion of women married in their early 20s (see Figure 8). Since then, the average age when a woman married for the first time increased from 20.8 years to 23.6 years. This increase is concurrent with women's increased levels of education and participation in the work force. In the 1990s, more women will marry in their late twenties as education, work, and family share equal priority. Counselors must recognize the complexity of women's choices. Understanding how work and career fit into the overall goals and obligations of women's lives will improve the ability of counselors to suggest meaningful career development strategies.

In particular, counselors should pay attention to different cultural values concerning marriage. Hispanic and white women 20 to 24 years old have somewhat similar marriage patterns—just over 30 percent of them were single in 1970, while in 1988 over 50 percent were single. Over one fourth of Hispanic women 25 to 29 years old were single in 1988—a large increase from 13.7 percent in 1970. This significant change in the pattern will continue in the 1990s. As more single young women enter the work force, they will be less constrained by the obligations of marriage or a family and will have more opportunities to achieve higher educational goals and develop careers and paths for employment beyond entry-level work.

More black women were single in all age groups in 1970 compared to both white and Hispanic women. This was still the trend in 1988. Thirty-six percent of black women 30 to 34 years old had never married in 1988—the largest percentage of single women for that age group. In the 1990s, marriage patterns for white and Hispanic women will become even more similar, while a larger share of black women will remain single.

Marriage and educational attainment will contribute to an increasing occupational division in the labor force. Women with more than a high school diploma will get better paying jobs with promise of a career. Those with less education will find job mobility difficult. Both married and single

Figure 8. Percent of Women Who Have Never Married by Age Group

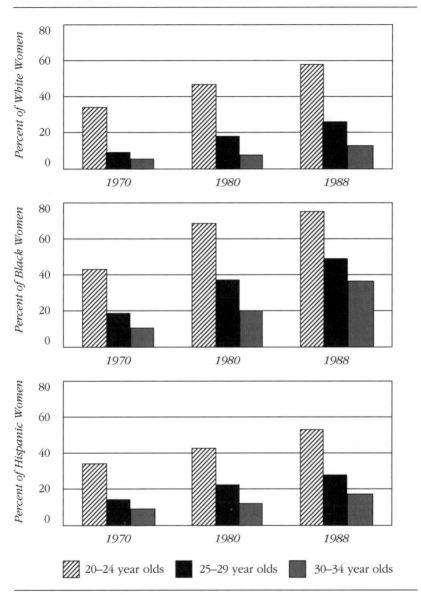

Source: U. S. Bureau of the Census, Current Population Reports, Series P-23, No. 162, *Studies in Marriage and the Family.*

**Figure 9. Labor Force Participation for Women
With Children Under 18 Years of Age**

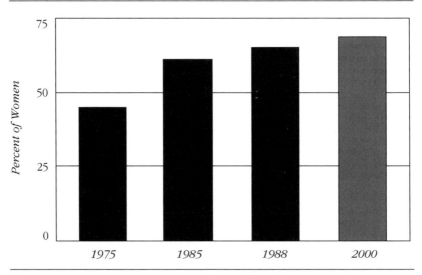

Source: IFTF; derived from historical data from the U.S. Department of Labor, Bureau of Labor Statistics, labor force statistics derived from the Current Population Survey, 1948–87, Table C–12.

women will participate in the labor force in the 1990s in greater numbers than they did in 1970. Less than half the married women 25 to 44 years old worked in 1970; however, in 1988 over two-thirds of them were in the work force.

Mothers in the Work Force. A key shift over the past three decades, and perhaps the single most important transformation of the 20th century, is the increase in the number of mothers who remain in the work force. In 1970, 4.5 million women with children under six years old worked, while by 1988 the number soared to 8 million. The number of employed mothers with children between 6 and 17 years old also increased tremendously from 7.3 million to 11.9 million. While single and divorced women with children traditionally have had high labor force participation rates, married women with children have not. Working mothers in the 1990s will have tremendous family responsibilities and will seek support and flexibility from their employers (see Figure 9). This trend will peak in the 1990s as more women of childbearing age enter the work force and as women who postponed childbearing during the 1970s and 1980s stay in the work force and have children.

Figure 10. Share of Total First Births to Women by Age Group

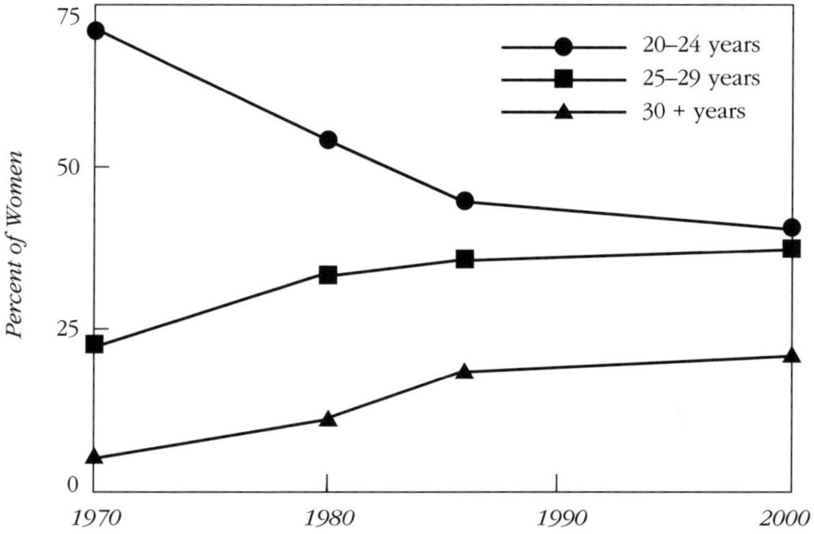

Source: IFTF; historical data from the U.S. National Center for Health Statistics, *Vital Statistics of the U.S.,* 1988, p. 19, Table 7.

More women in the 1990s will continue to postpone having their first child. The later a woman has a child, the more likely she is to stay in the labor force or take off only a brief period of time after the birth. In 1970, more than 70 percent of first births were to women 20 to 24 years old. By 1986, more women waited until they were older. In the year 2000, more than 20 percent of first-born children will be to women older than 30 (see Figure 10).

Women work for a number of different reasons—some to develop a career, some for extra income, and some for economic survival. It is important for counselors to explore a woman's key reasons and motivations to work. This will improve the relevance of career choices in specific industries and occupations.

Participation of Women Workers in the 1990s. In the 1990s, the participation of all women in the work force probably will peak by the end of the decade at about 63 percent. The participation of prime-aged women (25–44 years old), however, will peak at a little over 80 percent. The women who will contribute to the increase are:

▶ *Working mothers.* More women aged 25 to 34 will have children but continue to work. The majority will be white and will work in supervisory or managerial levels.

▶ *Women reentering the labor force.* Women aged 35 to 54 will return to the labor force after their children start school. Depending on their educational levels, they will work either in clerical, sales, and administrative support positions or reenter the professional ranks they left behind.

▶ *Young ethnic women.* Many young and poorly educated ethnic women will be employed in the growing service sector, while a small number of professionally and technically skilled ethnic women workers will work in supervisory and managerial positions.

▶ *Women managers less likely to be single or childless.* Employers cannot assume that women in the work force of 2000 will have decided to forego marriage or children for economic reasons or for career aspirations as they did in the past. Studies of female managers and supervisors reveal that 50 percent or more of 40-year-olds are not married and as much as 90 percent of older management-level women do not have children. These percentages will decrease in the 1990s. Employer strategies that support choice and flexibility will make the best use of the educated and trained mothers who do not want to leave the work force.

▶ *Women who are members of dual-earning couples.* More than two-thirds of married couples with children will be two-job families. These working couples will have heightened family responsibility to children as well as to elderly parents.

Career counselors should assist women workers through simulated job interviews and role playing in learning how to respond to employers' questions about family issues and how to question employers about their policies toward workers with family responsibilities. In the past, this area has been a controversial item in interviews. Today it is a central work issue. Counselors may want to start developing a data base of jobs and employers who have made room for family responsibilities in the workplace.

Hispanics in the Labor Force

As workers retire and leave, the new workers who replace them will bring about a dramatic shift in the ethnic composition of the labor force. A careful look at the total number of men and women entering and leaving the work force reveals a more accurate picture of new (net) workers during the next decade.

Figure 11. Projected Net Growth in Labor Force by Group, 1988–2000

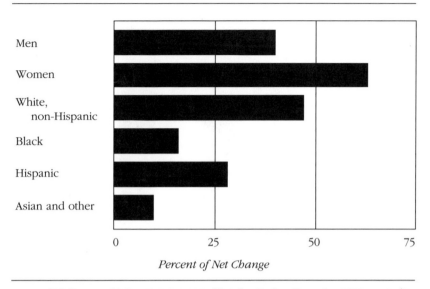

Percent of Net Change

Source: U.S. Bureau of Labor Statistics, *Monthly Labor Review,* November 1989, pp. 3–65

Women will make up 62 percent of the net growth in the labor force. While approximately two-thirds of the entrants are white, an overwhelming 83 percent of workers leaving are also white and more than half of them men. As a result, women, blacks, Hispanics, and Asians will make up the majority of labor force growth.

Of the ethnic subgroups in the work force, Hispanics will account for the most growth in the future labor market—they will represent over 27 percent of the net growth (see Figure 11). Although Hispanics accounted for only 7.3 percent of the total labor force in 1988, there will be more new workers from Hispanic cultures than from any other ethnic group in the next decade. The latter part of the decade will see tremendous Hispanic labor force growth whose numbers will reach over 14 million by 2000 (see Figure 12). A key challenge for career development professionals is to determine how Hispanics' language, culture, and educational backgrounds differ and to distinguish their participation in the labor force from other workers.

Demographic Factors. The Hispanic share of the U.S. population has increased rapidly because of high fertility rates among women and a high level of immigration. From 1982 to 1987, the total number of Hispanics increased by over 22 percent, compared to a 6.8 percent increase in the U.S. population. The U.S. Bureau of the Census estimates Hispanics will make

Figure 12. Hispanics in the Civilian Labor Force, 1976–2000

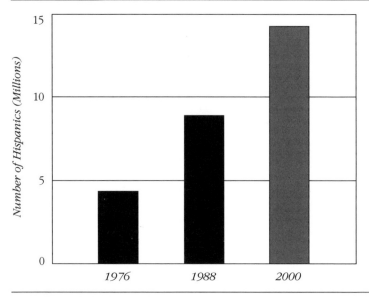

Source: U.S. Bureau of Labor Statistics, *Monthly Labor Review,* November 1989, pp. 3–65

up almost 9.5 percent of the total population in 2000. This corresponds to over 25 million people.

Hispanics are the youngest workers in the labor force. In 1988, their average age was 32.9 years—three years younger than the average of the total U.S. work force. Hispanics will remain the youngest workers in the 1990s, even as their average age increases to 35.2—4.1 years younger than the median age for the total labor force. The increasing age gap between Hispanics and the rest of the work force reflects the rapid aging of white workers—median age of 39.6 years.

Immigration is a significant factor in the growing number of Hispanics in the labor force. The Census Bureau reports that an average of 250,000 legal Hispanic immigrants arrive each year, the majority of them in California. In addition, an estimated 200,000 immigrants arrive illegally, most of them from Mexico, the Caribbean, and Central America. Whether the Immigration Reform and Control Act (IRCA) of 1986 limits the number of illegals entering the United States depends on whether employers abide by it, or if they don't, whether fines are effective deterrents to hiring illegals. Some employers admit that they refrain from hiring anyone who looks Hispanic, has a Hispanic surname, or speaks little English to avoid hassles and possible fines by the Immigration and Naturalization Service (INS) officials. Others continue to hire immigrants, hoping they are working legally. Factors such as the levels of economic growth and stability in Mexico and continuing political turmoil and violence in Central America influence the number of immigrants entering the United States both legally and illegally. The relevance and effectiveness of the IRCA legislation may vary according to such external factors.

Economic and political conditions in Mexico and Central America have significant impact on the daily experiences and the emotional and cultural background acquired by these potential workers—many of whom have witnessed extreme violence and hardship. This is particularly true for youths and young children, who had to learn survival strategies in a hostile environment during their formative years. The manifestations of these experiences while at work or in school in the United States only now are acknowledged as a serious issue to be addressed by educators and employers. It will remain a serious issue in the coming decade as immigration continues. Career counselors can play a large role in dealing with this issue for a large portion of their clients. Some workers may be reluctant to approach employers aggressively or to reveal much about their background (including skills and work experience) because of a violent and unstable history. Counselors will need to help such job seekers break down these barriers and learn how to demonstrate their strengths in the work force.

Participation Rates. The participation rate of Hispanics increased significantly since 1976, moving from the second lowest (compared to other ethnic and racial groups) to the highest in the 1990s (see Figure 13). Part of this growth is driven by a 9 percent increase in Hispanic women's labor force participation between 1976 and 1988. Hispanic women's participation will further increase by 6.2 percent by 2000, heavily contributing to the overall Hispanic participation rate.

Hispanic women may respond to different guidance strategies and support from career counselors than other women in the labor force because of cultural differences. Counselors should identify early on the expectations Hispanic women have of the workplace and how they can help Hispanic women work without offending any cultural or moral values concerning obligations to family and children.

Education. Educational attainment is one of the most important factors for employment and job mobility. Yet traditionally, attainment levels have been lower for Hispanics than non–Hispanics and their high school dropout rate has been higher. In California, for example, the 1988–1989 dropout rate for all Hispanic students in public high school was 28.5

Figure 13. Labor Force Participation Rates
by Ethnic and Racial Group, 1976–2000

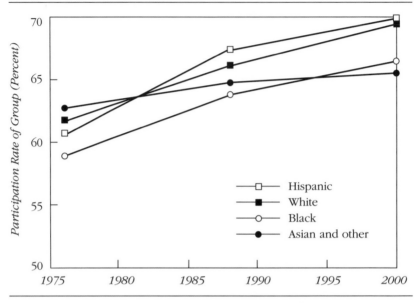

Source: IFTF; derived from historical data from the U.S. Bureau of Labor Statistics, *Monthly Labor Review*, August 1988 and November 1989.

percent, compared to 20.4 percent for non–Hispanics. The rate of college completion among Hispanics is about half that of non–Hispanics.

Younger Hispanics, however, have a higher educational attainment level than older Hispanics. Hispanics 25 to 34 years old are much more likely to have finished high school than those older than 35. By the year 2000, more children of Hispanics with high school diplomas will complete high school and go on to college, raising the educational level of the Hispanic base in the labor force. The ratio of U.S.-born to non–U.S.-born Hispanics will be larger because indigenous Hispanic population growth will contribute more to labor force growth than immigration. According to the Bureau of Labor Statistics, U.S.-born Hispanics have more than two years more schooling than Hispanics born outside the United States and earn about $2,000 more per year. This means a better educated and upwardly mobile labor pool in the future. It also implies that counselors need to target immigrant children at school to raise their attainment levels to those of children born in the United States.

It is important for counselors to stress skill acquisition and education as a strategy for Hispanics planning careers. This may be difficult for Hispanic women with stressful family obligations. Counselors may want to identify occupations where there is a better opportunity for on-the-job training rather than off-site, after-hours training programs, which may be difficult for such women to attend regularly.

Language. Language is a sign of ethnic heritage and identity, but it can also be a barrier for mobility in U.S. society. Several states, California among them, have passed legislation that designates English as the official language. Voting material, registration material, and public signs and messages, including those in the workplace, are to be communicated in English. This may be an obstacle for Hispanics and other limited-English speakers in the future job market.

Most language and ethnic studies researchers agree that language is one of the best indicators of ethnic identity but also one of the hardest to fully understand because of its relationship to social life. Several studies concur that proficiency in English is related to age; older groups tend to report lower levels of proficiency, while younger groups rate their Spanish proficiency low and the English higher. Some surveys report that by the second generation, the number of couples reporting Spanish as their home language falls from 84 percent to 15 percent. During the 1990s, more Hispanic families will speak English in their homes because there will be more second- and third-generation families in the total population. This will increase the amount of English-speaking Hispanics in public schools and in the workplace, reducing the language barriers that contribute to limited performance and mobility.

Career counselors will need to help limited-English speakers find ways to improve their English. In addition to identifying specific programs for English instruction, counselors should develop a network of progressive employers who are aware of the need to accommodate limited-English speaking workers with English programs and policies that do not penalize workers based on language deficiency. Counselors should point out to their clients—as well as to employers—that job interviews, performance evaluations, and other types of job screenings most likely will be conducted in English. While these procedures may demonstrate a worker's limited proficiency in English, they may not adequately reflect a worker's talent, ability to learn, and true professional ability.

Strategies to Reach New Workers

Looking at specific subgroups in the work force such as women and Hispanics demonstrates that workers will have a great diversity of needs now and in the next decade. Referring to subgroups as "minorities" is inaccurate and will underestimate their needs. Key implications for counselors and other career development professionals are outlined below.

▶ *Reevaluate training priorities.* Traditional training will need careful reevaluation. Current training programs may not be adequate to address new large groups within the labor force. Counselors may need to start or upgrade programs in basic education, English, and job skills in order to provide all employees with the tools to be productive. Certain modes of delivery—such as classroom-based instruction, videotapes, self-paced study, and so forth—may be most effective on specific groups of workers in particular settings.

▶ *Devise new standards.* Since future workers will have such different backgrounds and work experiences, standardization of certain work processes may contain biases that prevent potential workers from performing at their true proficiency level. Job performance evaluations, assessments for job mobility, and rewards and penalties cannot be guided by antiquated assumptions. Many assumptions that held true in prior decades when white males accounted for most of the labor force will not be appropriate. Career advisors will need to help workers find new ways to demonstrate their skills and overcome potential obstacles to their job advancement.

▶ *Meet special needs of ethnic workers.* Special training and education on the job and associated programs with local high schools and community colleges should target the needs of ethnic women workers. They will be part of a valuable strategy to facilitate work force participation and job mobility. Counselors could play a key role in linking high schools, community colleges, and local employers. Because of the smaller pool of new workers in the future, employers will seek out career counselors and other nontraditional sources to find qualified workers.

▶ *Reach out to the nontraditional work force.* Employers as well as educators and counselors will need to establish links with communities and local organizations to deliver training to disenfranchised workers. Community outreach to specific groups such as youths, older workers, single mothers, and working couples will help integrate these workers into the work force. One good example of this is the school-business partnership. Schools, including K through 12, vocational schools, and two-year colleges, and businesses are connecting with each other in creative ways to help the transition from school to work. Learning more about the community environment will shed light on particular needs of workers and mechanisms to address them. The role of career development specialists will become more central in the education and the work community of the future as they focus on building informational links among workers, employers, and trainers.

Occupational Change in the 1990s

In the 1990s, work will be transformed by increased use of information technology and by the trend toward continued organizational restructuring. As a result, there will be distinct occupational shifts in several industries. An understanding of the job growth and decline in industries will provide counselors with a richer context for developing employment and career strategies.

In the 1990s, the job market will become increasingly polarized based on skill and education. Approximately 12.8 million new jobs will be created in the next decade. This is equivalent to less than 1 percent job growth per year in the 1990s—much slower than in the 1970s or 1980s. Opportunities for high-paying jobs will be limited to those with high levels of education and demonstrated skill, either through past job experience or appropriate training. Available low-skill jobs will be comparatively low-paying and offer little chance for advancement or job mobility. This is a major characteristic of the job market that counselors must acknowledge and communicate to their clients.

The Shift to a Service-producing Economy

Eighty-four percent of the new jobs in the next decade (10.8 million) will be in the service sector—primarily in retail trade, services, and the government. Technology will have a particularly strong impact on these three sectors and will widen the gap between sophisticated, high-skilled jobs and low-skilled jobs. Managers will find it more difficult to manage a two-tiered work force. It will be more difficult to communicate corporate goals and to establish a consistent corporate culture in a work force with great variation in skill levels. Young entry-level workers without fundamental training in analysis, decision making, and communication skills (both oral and written) will find the job market extremely limited.

The goods-producing sector will grow by only 0.1 percent during the 1990s, and its share of total employment will further shrink to 18.1 percent from 25.2 percent in 1980. Jobs in the manufacturing industry, the largest segment of the goods-producing industry, will decrease by 0.1 percent (about 100,000 jobs), yet this segment still will account for a third of the total dollar output of all industries (see Figure 14).

The shrinking numbers of jobs in the goods-producing sector does not mean manufacturing will be less important to the economy. There will be significant occupational shifts, however, where workers will be doing different tasks. Technology will substitute for many of the routine production and operations jobs. That will allow workers to take on new information-oriented responsibilities involving analysis and decision making. New recruits in these industries will have to demonstrate more sophisticated

Figure 14. Number of Jobs in Major Industry Sectors, 1970–2000

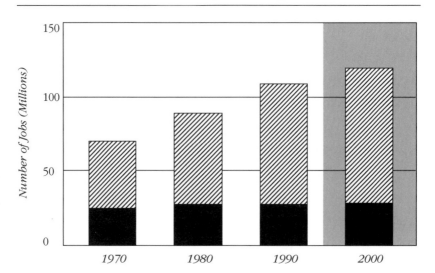

Service-producing   Goods-producing

Source: IFTF; derived from historical data from the U.S. Bureau of Labor Statistics, *Monthly Labor Review*, November 1989, and the U.S. Department of Commerce, *U.S. Statistical Abstract*, 1990, Table No. 651.

skills in order to match the new job requirements. There will be fewer jobs, for example, in machine setting and operating and in assembling and fabricating. The smaller number of available new jobs will be in machine repair or support positions that require a broader understanding of overall operations in a plant and a greater ability to make decisions based on a variety of different information supplied by new technology.

The shift to a service-producing economy creates two major challenges in the 1990s. First, employers must learn how to increase and maintain productivity in an economy where there is a shift from a focus on production of the product to a focus on servicing the customer with the product. This increases the organization's concern over product delivery and how it meets the needs and perceptions of customers. This is true for both the service-producing industries and the goods-producing industries.

As technology streamlines production tasks, workers increasingly will find themselves in positions that focus on learning about customer needs, customer perceptions, and how to differentiate their products with value-added services. Jobs in finance and insurance, for example, will require more customized services and the development of niche markets. Computers and telecommunications technologies will reduce the information bottlenecks typically caused by slow manual recording, retrieving, and data manipulation that made these tasks more difficult and time consuming to accomplish and reserved them for middle-level managers. Production, operations, and other nonmanagement workers will be relieved of routine tasks and given coordination activities. They'll be asked to use new applications of technology based on accessible information. Workers will have more information about the production process and about customers to analyze and interpret in order to make operations and marketing decisions. Quality service as well as a quality product will be a high priority in the 1990s.

Career counselors must appreciate the importance of this new service orientation and view the production process as an ongoing process of evaluation and improvement. Professionals working in career development face the challenge of communicating employers' goals to potential employees and helping them develop techniques to demonstrate they are capable of working in the new workplace.

A related challenge for career counselors is to help workers find appropriate and relevant training programs and workplace orientation so that they share the corporate culture of high-quality customer service and customer focus. Counselors also may find it useful to communicate with human resource professionals in order to learn about new organizational processes and policies designed to help workers use information to make decisions about quality, production processes, and customers. Educating workers about customer service and how to use information to formulate service strategies may be difficult if workers have a wide range of skills, abilities, and needs. Counselors should stress the importance of learning information-management skills to workers looking for employment in service and goods-producing industries. These skills include decision making, reading comprehension, writing, critical thinking, reasoning, and good listening habits. All of these skill areas can be facilitated with technology, yet developing them is not dependent on sophisticated information technology.

Fast Growth Industries With Large Employment Bases

The most dynamic job restructuring will take place in industries with high growth and large employment. These industries will experience profound occupational shifts and greater segmentation of workers based on their education level and experience. For this reason, it is important that the work force subgroups, identified in the first part of the chapter, understand the value of higher levels of educational attainment, skill acquisition, and demonstrated work responsibility. These are the attributes that employers will be looking for in new workers.

Table 2. Number of Jobs in Major Industries, 1980–2000

	1980	1990	2000
Goods-producing	25.7	25.2	**25.5**
Mining	1.0	0.6	**0.6**
Construction	4.3	5.3	**5.7**
Manufacturing	20.3	19.2	**19.1**
Service-producing	64.4	84.1	**94.9**
Transportation and utilities	5.1	5.6	**5.9**
Wholesale trade	5.3	6.2	**6.8**
Retail trade	15.0	20.3	**22.6**
Finance, insurance, and real estate	5.2	7.1	**7.8**
Services	17.5	27.3	**33.2**
Government	16.2	17.7	**18.6**
Agriculture	3.4	3.3	**3.0**
Private households	1.3	1.2	**1.1**
Nonfarm self-employed and unpaid family	7.3	9.1	**9.7**

Note: Numbers may not add up due to rounding.

Source: IFTF; derived from historical data from the U.S. Bureau of Labor Statistics, *Monthly Labor Review,* November 1989, and the U.S. Department of Commerce, U. S. Statistical Abstract, 1990, Table No. 651.

In the 1990s, the services—health, business, personal, and recreational—will continue to be the largest and fastest growing sector, with an average annual rate of 2.0 percent, although slower than the rate in the 1970s and the 1980s. Finance, insurance, and real estate will be the second fastest growing source of jobs (see Figure 15).

Retail trade (another major segment of the service-producing sector) will grow more slowly in the 1990s (1%), but it will surpass the manufacturing industry by 3.5 million jobs. Retail trade will replace manufacturing as the second largest source of jobs after the services (see Table 2). It will become the last major source of jobs for the unskilled and least marketable workers; however, many retail jobs also will be upgraded with increased use of technology. The small number of new manufacturing jobs will require high skill levels and no longer will be a source of employment for workers with only a high school diploma or less.

The services and retail trade segments of the service-producing sector will add 5.9 million and 2.3 million jobs, respectively, to the economy— a total of 55.8 million jobs by 2000. Together they will make up 64 percent of new job growth and 41 percent of total employment by 2000. Services alone will contribute to almost half of new employment by 2000 (see Table 2).

Figure 15. Employment Growth Rates in the 1990s

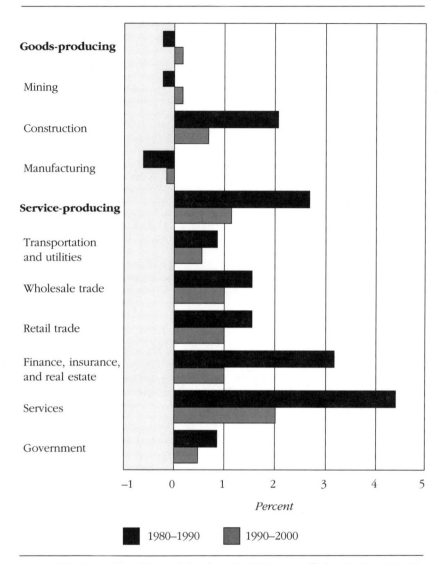

Source: IFTF; derived from historical data from the U.S. Bureau of Labor Statistics, *Monthly Labor Review,* November 1989, and the U.S. Department of Commerce, *U.S. Statistical Abstract,* 1990, Table No. 651.

Table 3. Number of Jobs in Selected Service Industries, 1970–2000 (Millions)

	1980	1990	2000
Health Services	5.3	7.8	**10.1**
Offices of health practitioners	1.2	2.1	**2.8**
Nursing and personal care facilities	1.0	1.4	**1.9**
Hospitals, private	2.8	3.4	**4.2**
Outpatient facilities, health services n.e.c.*	0.3	0.9	**1.2**
Business Services**	3.1	6.5	**8.3**
Services to dwellings and other buildings	0.5	0.9	**1.0**
Personnel supply services	0.6	1.7	**2.2**
Computer and data processing	0.3	0.8	**1.2**
Research, management, and consulting	0.5	0.9	**1.2**

* n.e.c. = not elsewhere classified
** includes Business Services not listed

Source: IFTF; derived from historical data from the U.S. Bureau of Labor Statistics, *Monthly Labor Review,* November 1989, and the U.S. Department of Commerce, *U.S. Statistical Abstract,* 1990, Table No. 651.

Small employment growth in a large industry translates into substantial employment opportunities. Fast-growing employment in a small industry, on the other hand, may mean higher employment potential but stiffer competition since more workers will be competing for a relatively small number of jobs. The 0.1 percent decline of the manufacturing industry, for example, may belie the fact that it still employs over 19 million workers. However, there will be greater competition for the smaller number of new jobs. The government sector is projected to grow only 0.5 percent, but this translates into an additional one million jobs and will almost equal manufacturing in the total number employed.

Health and Business Service Industries. Jobs in health care, medical facilities, and support and maintenance of hospitals and business organizations are increasingly data- and information-based. The health care industry, for example, is adjusting to changes in the reimbursement methods and in the information and data required to feed the health care system (see Table 3).

Written and oral communications and analytical and problem-solving skills will be basic requirements for most jobs as imaging, storage, and data-transmission technologies increase the flow and quality of information in these jobs. Some service positions related to business and health will not require advanced training. However, these jobs will be low paying and typically less than full-time. Turnover will be high, and it will be difficult for workers to learn more sophisticated skills necessary for higher paying jobs. As employers use job experience and training to screen new workers in these areas, advancement will be restricted.

Retail Trade Industry. Retail is the second largest source of new employment in the service-producing sector, with almost 23 million jobs. Labor-intensive jobs at eating and drinking establishments will make up more than half of the new retail trade job growth (1.5 million jobs). Other industries with high projected growth and large employment bases in the 1990s are grocery stores, department stores, and miscellaneous shopping goods stores. These all have projected growth rates equal to or higher than the average growth of total employment.

Traditionally, youths have filled the occupations in retail trade, turning it into a haven for part-time work with high turnover. Technology developments such as innovations in food preparation have reduced the skill requirements of some retail jobs and have made it easier for employers to manage a part-time work force. The use of technologies such as point-of-sale terminals, hand-held inventory devices, and other storage and data base technologies will polarize the retail industry. The smaller number of low-skilled retail jobs will employ those without education and skills—high school dropouts, immigrants with poor English, and those with no training. At the same time, jobs as supervisors and managers will become increasingly complex and more sophisticated. Young entry workers with skills will find opportunity in these higher skilled retail jobs, which will lead to better job mobility, higher salaries, and benefits. Employers will have to identify carefully where technology and training must be deployed to make the best use of the tighter labor market in order to remain productive and competitive.

Occupations Requiring High Skill Levels. Information technology and telecommunications will continue to allow organizations to work across locations, across time zones, and in new ways. All workers—young entry-level workers as well as experienced workers—will have to learn how to work in groups and teams that are supported by technology. Facsimile, electronic mail, sophisticated telephones, and more powerful and functional personal computers will continue to change the expectations of the ordinary white-collar office support worker or medical office assistant. Workers will be expected to perform more complex tasks within the work day. Hand-held computers for inventory recording will require stockroom and record-keeping workers to use new analytical and problem-solving skills because they will have both the access and the power to manipulate information. Consequently, the flow of information and the interaction among workers at the same location and at different locations will be increasingly dynamic.

Upgraded jobs will require more than a high school diploma and many will require advanced training and education. The largest contribution to new jobs in all industries will be in occupations that are service oriented (3.3 million). A high school diploma will be the minimum level of job preparation for a smaller percentage of service occupations. In 1988, 31 percent of workers in service occupations had less than a high school diploma. This percentage will dwindle to less than 10 percent by the year 2000. The percentage with some college will increase and raise the overall base level of education among workers in service occupations.

The job outlook for those with only a high school diploma is grim. In 1988, almost three-quarters of the workers in professional specialty occupations had four or more years of college. The majority of technical, marketing, and sales workers had some college education. This trend will continue in the 1990s.

The growth of professional, managerial, technical, and related support occupations will grow in synch with the high industry growth in the health and business services and in the finance, insurance, real estate, and government industries. Some college will be the minimal level of training required for these jobs, and the percentage of those with college will increase substantially (see Table 4).

In all occupations, however, employers will expect certain fundamental qualities from workers. Many employee attributes that employers deem critical are not content based, but have to do with a level of maturity and responsibility. Career counselors should stress that these skills, in addition to particular content or technical skills, are high on employers' lists. Some of the following are desirable attributes that employers find many new workers lack:

▶ Follow-through on assignments

▶ Ability to function cooperatively with co-workers

▶ Ability to accommodate to change—to shift tasks and settings

▶ Dependability

▶ Ability to write and speak effectively

▶ Pride in the quality of work

Table 4. Total Employment by Educational Attainment, March 1988

Occupation	Level of Growth	Percent of Total Employment for Occupation Based on Level of Education			
		Less Than High School	High School	One to Three Years of College	Four or More Years of College
Total, all occupations	Medium	16	40	21	23
Executive, administrative and managerial occupations	Medium	5	27	24	44
Professional specialty occupations	High	2	9	15	74
Technicians and related support occupations	High	3	29	36	32
Marketing and sales occupations	Medium	13	39	24	23
Administrative support occupations, including clerical	Low	7	51	30	12
Service occupations	High	31	45	18	6
Precision production, craft, and repaid occupations	Low	23	53	18	5
Operatives, fabricators, and laborers	Very Low	33	51	12	4
Agriculture, forestry, fishing, and related occupations	Decline	36	44	12	7

Source: U.S. Bureau of Labor Statistics, *Monthly Labor Review,* November 1989, Table 8.

▶ Ability to search, research, and apply information

▶ Concern for productivity

▶ The ability to follow instructions

▶ Ability to adapt to and use new information technologies

Conclusion

Helping both the worker and the workplace adapt to each other is a key goal for career counselors in the 1990s. A critical step toward achieving this is to research individual organizations' policies and programs to cooperatively integrate work force issues into their overall vision. Career counselors also should play a significant role in encouraging development of such policies. Career development professionals serve as important intermediaries in bridging the expectations of both workers and employers and helping them develop strategies that will satisfy their goals—employment for workers in a promising career and a qualified and motivated work force for employers.

The failure to adequately deal with future human resource issues now will result in continued incongruity between the type of jobs that will be created in the next decade and the caliber and orientation of workers. Workers and employers need to be prepared for a world of work that is in the process of dramatic transformation.

Workers' relationship to technology will become closer in the 1990s. Information technology and telecommunications will facilitate many work tasks in most jobs, enabling workers to increase their productivity and the value they bring to the work process. These technologies will enable the structure of work to change geographically and physically within an organization, and across time as well, given the 24-hour accessibility of information. The way workers use technology on the job as a tool also will increase their responsibility and accountability to the organization. Work will become more cooperative and team-based. The work environment will be increasingly more complex.

Identifying the critical basic skills for the 1990s must be the foundation of training and educational programs for workers in the next decade. Occupations that require workers to manipulate information and relate directly to people also will grow—this is true for the goods-producing industries as well. Vocational and academic programs should target effective communication, problem solving, and analytical skills as key goals. Learning will become an integrated aspect of work for *all* workers. On-the-job training will become a dated term as learning is embedded in daily work tasks. Knowing how to learn will be a highly valued attribute of workers in the 1990s.

List of Sources

Statistics in tables and figures were gathered from the sources listed below. IFTF derives its forecasts from historical data provided by these sources and its own internal sources.

U.S. Bureau of the Census. (1971). *Educational attainment in the United States: March 1970*(Current Population Reports, Series P–20, No. 207). Washington, DC: U.S. Government Printing Office.

U.S. Bureau of the Census. (1982). *Educational attainment in the United States: March 1981 and 1980* (Current Population Reports, Series P–20, No. 390). Washington, DC: U.S. Government Printing Office.

U.S. Bureau of the Census. (1982). *Studies in marriage and the family* (Current Population Reports, Series P–23, No. 162). Washington, DC: U.S. Government Printing Office.

U.S. Bureau of the Census. (1988). *Educational attainment in the United States: March 1987 and 1986* (Current Population Reports, Series P–20, No. 428). Washington, DC: U.S. Government Printing Office.

U.S. Department of Commerce. (1990). *Statistical abstract of the U.S.* Washington, DC: U.S. Government Printing Office.

U.S. Department of Labor, Bureau of Labor Statistics. (1988, March). Women and the labor market: The link grows stronger. *Monthly Labor Review, 111* (3), 3–8.

U.S. Department of Labor, Bureau of Labor Statistics. (1988, August). *Labor force statistics derived from the current population survey, 1948–1987* (Bulletin 2307). Washington, DC: U.S. Government Printing Office.

U.S. Department of Labor, Bureau of Labor Statistics. (1988, August). The growing presence of Hispanics in the U.S. workforce. *Monthly Labor Review, 111* (8), 9–14.

U.S. Department of Labor, Bureau of Labor Statistics. (1989, August). *Handbook of labor statistics* (Bulletin 2340). Washington, DC: U.S. Government Printing Office.

U.S. Department of Labor, Bureau of Labor Statistics. (1989, November). Outlook 2000. *Monthly Labor Review, 111* (8), 3–65.

U.S. Department of Labor, Bureau of Labor Statistics (1990, January). *Employment and earnings.* Washington, DC: U.S. Government Printing Office.

U.S. Department of Labor, Bureau of Labor Statistics. (1990, April). *Outlook 2000* (Bulletin 2352). Washington, DC: U.S. Government Printing Office.

U.S. National Center for Health Statistics. *Vital statistics of the U.S., 1988* (Table 7). Washington, DC: U.S. Government Printing Office.

Practical Exercises for Counselors

There are several tasks that counselors can do to assist their clients in developing strategies to begin or change careers. Some of these involve exercises with their clients, while others are tasks that counselors can do to help them manage and organize career information that they gather.

Counselors who are most informed and in touch with local employers will best serve their clients.

Practical Exercises With Clients

▶   *Simulated Interviews.* The ability to perform well in an interview is a critical job-hunting skill that is always useful. Many individuals looking for employment do not get the opportunity to practice this experience with an informed and skilled career professional. Practice interviews will help individuals hone their speaking, presentation, and listening skills. They also give job seekers self-confidence and reduce the uncertainty of what a job interview is all about. This will be a particularly beneficial exercise for young, first-time job hunters and women reentries to the work force who have no recent or relevant practice in this area. Individuals with different language and cultural backgrounds will benefit tremendously from the opportunity to practice a job interview with a true professional in a professional environment. Part of this session should include a résumé writing exercise.

▶   *Team Building Exercises.* More organizations are working in groups and teams. Workers who can demonstrate these skills and can express in interviews their understanding of what this work style means will be at an advantage. Counselors should look for ways to organize and run workshops or sessions at various convenient hours during the day and evening when their clients can go through these sessions, or invest in the training themselves so that they can run these sessions. Participants in these exercises will benefit from learning about cooperation, delegation of tasks, responsibility to the group, and other important team skills that are highly valued in the workplace. These exercises will be beneficial to first-time workers as well as experienced workers looking for a career change.

▶   *Target Educational Opportunities.* Counselors should stress with all their clients the importance of education for gaining employment, retaining their jobs, and improving their compensation. Counselors can help their clients review their skills and educational back-ground and suggest areas that may need improvement. They can suggest specific programs and courses at high schools, community colleges, and universities that would address their clients' educational and skill needs. Counselors should also stress that this process of reevaluating skills and education is an ongoing process in the workplace of the future.

Tasks for Counselors

▶ *Develop a Database of Progressive Employers.* Career counselors should compile their existing data and develop an ongoing collection of employers who are forward-thinking and take appropriate steps for dealing with the future worker. Employers who make room for work/family issues, have creative benefit plans, address the needs of ethnic workers, strategically employ older workers, and offer on-the-job training should be organized into a database. This may involve several databases organized by services or key characteristics of the employer or a single listing of employers and their human resource policies and practices. Capturing and organizing this information (much of which is public information) will help counselors match workers with potential employers.

▶ *Develop a Database of Educational Programs.* Counselors should perform ongoing collection and updating of relevant educational programs—both vocational and basic education. This will help counselors stay in touch with educators and build links with educational institutions, and it will provide workers with information about real options for educational improvement.

▶ *Develop a Network of Professionals.* Counselors should begin to develop a network of professionals, either potential employers or local professionals, who are willing to conduct informational interviews with job hunters. These interviews will present opportunities for job hunters to practice their interview skills with a real professional, and it will be an opportunity for them to learn more about the occupation or industry of the interviewer. This type of face-to-face interaction is invaluable for job hunters.

6

• • • • • • • •

Meeting the Needs
of the Multicultural Work Force

DAVID C. WIGGLESWORTH

A few decades ago Bob Dylan was singing "the times they are a-changing." Today, as we look at the ethnic and gender diversity in the work force, it is an all too obvious statement that has much significance for those in career development.

We know that the labor force is changing. The Hudson Institute's (1987) report entitled *Workforce 2000* clearly depicts the dramatic changes that we can expect in the work force in the 21st century. In 1985, white males comprised almost half of the labor force (47%) in the United States, but by the year 2000 they will represent only 15 percent. The remaining 85 percent will be composed of women, minorities, and immigrants. Twenty percent of these will be U.S–born nonwhites and 23 percent will be immigrants. The *San Francisco Chronicle* reported in a November 1989 article entitled "The New Immigrants" the recently documented U.S. government statistics that some 28 percent of the annual immigrants to the United States end up in professional management positions. The times certainly are changing.

We need not wait for the year 2000 to see these effects: Significant changes are affecting the 1990s work force right now. In an April 1990 article entitled "Changing California—The New Demographics," the *San Francisco Examiner* reported that in California some 15 percent of the work force is foreign born, and in the San Francisco Bay Area, this number increases to 33 percent. San Francisco can lay claim to being the most ethnically diverse region in the United States, and this diversity in the labor force, while heightened in California, has had a broad impact on other areas throughout the United States.

These demographic changes will have an impact on most phases of career development activities. From an organizational perspective, we need to be aware of the impact these demographic changes will have on affirmative action, equal opportunity employment, staff planning, succession planning, and performance appraisal. From the perspective of the individual, we need to be aware of this impact on assessment instrumentation, resource workshops, and career development workshops.

What does this mean for career development professionals? First, we need to recognize that the changing demographics of the work force will present career development professionals with a somewhat different client group in terms of ethnicity and gender; the clients will be coming from a more culturally diverse population. Knowing how to best meet the individual needs of this diverse population will present an unrivaled challenge for those entering the field of career development.

Second, in addition to working with an altered client base, career development professionals will need to be able to help both managers and those just entering the work force prepare for the needs of the changing work force by developing their awareness and skills to meet these new challenges.

In order for career development professionals to help their clients to become more employable, they will need to know the new requirements for success in the work force. Specifically, managers and employees should familiarize themselves with the cultures represented in the multiethnic work force and come to an understanding of how each other perceives, processes information, and responds. As Harris and Moran (1991) indicate, it will be important for professionals to learn, within the context of each culture, to

▶ Convey respect

▶ Personalize knowledge

▶ Show empathy

▶ Be nonjudgmental

▶ Develop role flexibility

▶ Demonstrate reciprocal concern

▶ Develop tolerance for ambiguity

Members of the U.S. work force are accustomed to working within a national cultural context and often fail to realize that people from other nations or ethnicities have different value systems that influence their perceptions, communication styles, basic understandings, and ways of responding. Additionally, recently arrived workers from other countries often have linguistic and ethnically determined behaviors that need to be understood.

This is not to deny that there are great areas of commonality between all people, and while some may find it hard to accept, we are more alike than we are different. Differences, however, are what tend to exacerbate difficult situations in the workplace. To be effective members of multicultural work forces we need to know how best to make sure that everyone *really* understands.

It is facile to say that this is the United States, that we do things our way, and that people from diverse cultures must adapt to the ways of the majority culture. Some amount of adaptation and adjustment is required. But in order for career development professionals to help both managers and employees enhance productivity, job-site safety, and career development, a knowledge of the cultural and ethnic factors that influence their environment is essential. Some of these factors are:

▶ Perception

▶ Physical distance

▶ Time factors

▶ Body language

▶ Listening and articulation

▶ High and low context

▶ Conflict

Perception

Our perception is our reality. What we see is real for us. It reflects our value system and stems in part from our cultural and ethnic background as is evident in the evolution of art and music from one decade to the next from our own particular generation or time.

Perception is reactive, historical, after the fact. We respond to what we see (or think we see) *after* it occurs. Perception is often a filter through which we construct our own reality.

We know that individuals perceive differently. The eye-witness accounts of automobile accidents are often at wide variance with one another. In a psychology classroom experiment where someone enters the room and pretends to shoot the professor, the students' reports vary widely as to what actually happened.

Such perceptual differences become compounded when working with individuals from different cultures. Their frames of reference are different, as are their perceptual values. Rubenstein (1975) asks representatives from both Western and Eastern cultures how they would react if they were traveling on an ocean liner with their spouse, their child, and their mother and the ship began to sink. If they could save only one person other than themselves, who would it be? In the group from the Western culture, 60 percent said they would save the child and 40 percent the spouse. No one chose the mother. In the group from the Eastern culture, no one chose to save the child or the spouse—100 percent said they would save the mother. This dramatic example demonstrates the fact that people in different cultures have different perceptual values. Knowing something about how the members of a culturally diverse work force perceive would seem to be good advice for career development professionals.

Thus, a career counselor working with individuals from a specific ethnicity needs to research the values of that particular group to get an understanding of the factors that may affect their ways of perceiving. There is also the need for the counselor to cross-check the client's responses to questions that require more than a yes or no response in order to insure that their judgment of the client's perceptions are accurate.

Physical Distance

The role that physical distance plays in relation to communication, authority, and power must also be considered. In this country, we tend to act as if we have a bubble around our bodies that extends about two inches beyond our skin. If anyone breaks the bubble, they must apologize. In other cultures touching, holding hands, and embracing are customary, even among members of the same sex.

As Hofstede (1984) has demonstrated, there are also cultural imperatives to authority and power that reflect the role of physical distance between one's boss and one's self. This may also be true in relationships between career counselors and their clients.

Career development professionals need to understand the role that distance plays in the cultures of their clients.

Time Factors

The Latin time sense and its so-called mañana philosophy or the Zen concept of limitless time contrast sharply with our own sense of past, present, and future and the concept of saving, wasting, making up, or spending time.

In the United States we say that there is a time and place for everything. However, compared to people from other cultures, we do not always practice what we preach. Business, for example, is almost a universal value that can be discussed almost anytime or anywhere. People from other cultures may be more sensitive about the right time and place for an interaction.

Again, it is incumbent upon the career counselor to consider whether a client's tardiness for an appointment or failure to appear may be a manifestation of that client's culture. Perhaps in this case, the career counselor can help the client realize the importance of time in our culture and its applications within the work force community.

Body Language

The total impact of any message on a receiver is based 7 percent on the words used, 38 percent on how the words are said (tone of voice, volume, inflection), and 55 percent on nonverbal factors such as facial expressions, hand gestures, body position, and eye contact (Hofstede, 1984).

One problem in an ethnically diverse work force is that gestures have different meanings in different cultures. The "A-OK" gesture that to us means that things are fine or great, or that something has been understood perfectly, is considered obscene in Brazil, has monetary connotations to the Japanese, and means zilch or zero to the French. Thumbs up in some Middle Eastern cultures is the equivalent of the extended third finger in the United States. Crossing the index and third fingers, which symbolizes a wish for good luck in our culture, suggests a desire for sexual intercourse in some Southeast Asian cultures. Other natural gestures may convey something other than their intended meanings to people from other cultures. Or we may miss significant communication cues because the gestures of another culture have no meaning in the American culture. For example, when a Japanese scratches his head, sucks in his breath, and says "*sah*," it indicates that he is not understanding the discussion. It is important for the career counselor to be aware of these problems.

Eye contact can also create problems. In the United States, looking someone in the eye conveys a sense of trustworthiness. We tend to believe that this applies to all cultures. Yet in parts of Asia and West Africa and in the culture of many Black Americans, looking someone in the eye is taboo, often inviting a hostile reaction.

Listening and Articulation

As children, the first communication skill we learn is listening. Next we learn to speak, then read, and finally, to write. This natural progression of learning communication skills corresponds to the way we use these skills in society. In school, however, this is reversed: We spend most of our time writing, then reading, then speaking, and last, listening (Hofstede, 1984). Yet we need to have finely tuned listening skills, especially for cross-cultural communication. A lack of understanding of cultural differences in communication can endanger both productivity and safety within the organization and can hinder our effectiveness as counselors.

Another point is the fact that different cultures have different linguistic patterns that can impact articulation. For example, people who come from cultures where there is no direct word for "no" are unlikely to use the word even in English, while individuals whose native language lacks an imperative verb form are not likely to be comfortable giving or receiving orders. In these instances, career counselors might do well to work in the realm of suggestions and to prepare their clients for the important role that the imperative verb form plays in the work force of this country.

High and Low Context

Edward Hall (1989) discusses the concept of high and low context within cultures. People from low-context cultures, such as in the English-speaking world, Germany, and Scandinavia, rely on information that is in explicit codes such as words. Meaning and understanding are focused on sending and receiving accurate messages directly, usually by being articulate with words and "spelling it all out."

People from high-context cultures, which is the rest of the world, rely on information that is either in the physical context or internalized in the person. Meaning and understanding are found in what is not spoken—in the nonverbal communication or body language, in the silences and pauses, and in relationships and empathy. People in high-context cultures communicate in other ways than by stating things.

The implication is that a high-context culture requires more conformance in behavior and allows for less deviation in role performance, whereas a low-context culture allows for more deviance from an ideal role enact-ment and thus tends to have more relaxed social structures. Further, the emotional-based, person-oriented approach characteristic of high-context cultures leads to strong interpersonal bonds between individuals, creating a tendency to allow for considerable bending of individual interests for the sake of the relationship. In low-context cultures, where the functionally based, explicit approach is taken, the interpersonal bond is generally seen as more fragile, indicated by the way that people in such cultures withdraw relatively easily from relationships that are not developing satisfactorily.

Career development professionals from low-context cultures interacting with clients from high-context cultures need to be aware that the very fundamentals of the basis for their communication are in opposition. The client may be uncomfortable with the explicitness of the conversation and miss key points. On the other hand, because the client communicates in apparent indirectness, the career counselor may not be able to fully understand the client and counsel ineffectively.

The critical factors discussed above suggest that when counselors communicate with clients from other cultures, clients may not find their expectations being met. The normal cues will not be forthcoming, and there will be misunderstandings. Where this is the case, it will have a negative impact on counseling and a detrimental effect on productivity, job-site safety, and the professional growth and development of individuals in the workplace. It is critical that we recognize these issues in order to promote the positive forces in our counseling.

As career development professionals, we need to understand ourselves and the role that personal factors in our lives—our education, our values, and our interpersonal abilities in familiar and new situations—play in our counseling abilities. We need to assess our degree of ethnocentrism and to realize that what may seem fair, reasonable, or logical to us may not seem so to members of a diverse work force. We need to be aware of the values of others and to avoid generic grouping of individuals who, while members of a particular ethnic group, are unique as individuals.

It is important to remember that there are also factors beyond culture that may influence behavior. It is sometimes convenient to conclude that a problem occurrence is due to cultural or linguistic differences when, in fact, it may be due to other causes. For example, a career counselor intent on increasing the upward mobility of a client who is satisfied where he or she is at in the corporate hierarchy may ascribe the client's "problem" to cultural or linguistic communication differences rather than to the counselor's own misevaluation of the client's personal goal.

Conflict

Conflict is perceived differently in high-context and low-context cultures (Hall & Hall, 1990). You will recall that the United States is considered a low-context culture and that most of the multicultural work force in this country represents a high-context culture.

One aspect of conflict that differs between these two types of cultures is the basis of or reason for the conflict. We know that conflict arises from either *instrumental* or *expressive* sources. Expressive conflicts arise from a desire to release tension, usually generated from hostile feelings, while instrumental conflict stems from a difference in goals or practices.

Low-context cultures tend to use analytic, linear logic and therefore are more likely to perceive conflict as instrumental rather than expressive; high-context cultures tend to use holistic, spiral logic and perceive conflict more as expressive than instrumental.

Another aspect of conflict differing across cultures relates to the conditions under which conflict occurs. In low-context cultures, conflict is likely to occur when an *individual's* expectations of appropriate behavior are being violated, as opposed to high-context cultures where the *group's* normative expectations of behavior are what is considered important. The rationale for this can be found in the role of context in providing information in these two types of cultures.

In low-context cultures, context plays a minor role because more information is spelled out in the message, whereas in the high-context cultures, context plays a crucial role in providing meaning to the message. Thus, the less important the context is, the more frequently violations of individual expectations lead to conflict. When context is important, violation of collective normative expectations may lead to conflict.

The attitude of the participant toward coping with conflict is another aspect of conflict that differs in low-context and high-context cultures. In low-context cultures, there is a direct approach to conflict that probably originates in the "doing" orientation and the reliance on linear logic, which leads to a confrontational attitude. In high-context cultures, there is an indirect attitude toward conflict that has its origins in a strong desire for group harmony and a reliance on indirect forms of communication, which leads to a nonconfrontational approach to conflict.

If career counselors can discover the conditions under which conflict arises in another culture and understand that culture's attitude toward conflict and its style of communication in the resolution of conflict, then they can increase their ability to correctly interpret and predict behavior in conflict situations and are more likely to successfully resolve the conflict. In some Far Eastern cultures, conflict is to be avoided at almost any cost and ignored if it should occur. Helping such clients to understand the role of conflict in our culture and to offer training in conflict resolution from our country's perspective will contribute to their more successful integration into the U.S. workplace.

As career development professionals, we may need to build our knowledge of management, remembering that management is personal, often one-on-one, and that it involves communication—upward, lateral, and downward. It involves guidelines, policies, and procedures. There are safe and correct ways of manufacturing, and there are the elements of the corporate culture that influence how things are accomplished in an organization. These guidelines, policies, procedures, ways of manufacturing, and elements of the corporate culture are communicated personally. The most effective professional managers are those who can maintain and enhance production while insuring the safety of their employees and giving them opportunities for personal growth and development as well as upward mobility.

From the individual's perspective, career development specialists can apply these considerations to such areas as assessment instrumentation, resource workshops, and career development workshops. Within an organizational framework, these considerations can be applied to the articulation of effective affirmative action and equal economic opportunity programs, to performance appraisal and succession planning, and to staff planning.

Within the organization, the specifics of organizational culture might be addressed by career developers through several means: (a) mentoring (or buddy-system) programs that allow for cross-cultural exchanges and learning, (b) mini–case studies in orientation programs, (c) culture-to-culture programs for major ethnic groups within an organization, (d) organizational professional development programs that have intercultural facets woven into the programs, and (e) organizational development process approaches to career development endeavors.

It is clear that for career counselors and career development professionals, enhancing the career development of a changing population and the management of diversity requires the acquisition of new skills that are appropriate to the needs of both managers and employees in the changing work force. In summary, they are

▶ Awareness of the cultural diversity in the work force

▶ Awareness of our own values and value systems

▶ Knowledge of the culture of others

▶ Ability to apply the knowledge and insights into other cultures to our profession

References

Changing California—The new demographics. (1990, April). *San Francisco Examiner,* p. 4.

Hall, E. T. (1989). *The basic works of Edward T. Hall: Vol. 1. The silent language; Vol. 2. The hidden dimension; Vol. 3. Beyond culture: The dance of life.* New York: Bantam/Doubleday.

Hall, E. T., & Hall, M. R. (1990). *Understanding cultural differences.* Yarmouth, ME: Intercultural Press.

Harris, P., & Moran, R. (1991). *Managing cultural differences.* Houston, TX: Gulf Publishing Co.

Hofstede, G. (1984). *Culture's consequences: International differences in work-related values.* Beverly Hill, CA: Sage.

The Hudson Institute. (1987). *Workforce 2000: Work and workers for the twenty-first century.* Indianapolis, IN: Author.

The New Immigrants. (1989, November). *San Francisco Chronicle,* p. 7.

Rubenstein, M. F. (1975). *Patterns of problem solving.* Englewood Cliffs, NJ: Prentice-Hall.

Exercises

Working with a culturally diverse work force is a new challenge for managers. Preparing people to work in a more diverse society is a new challenge for career development professionals. Let us try to apply some of the lessons from this chapter to the following discussion questions. The questions are designed to promote active discussions of the issues involved.

Discussion Question # 1

You are a career development professional working for a Japanese company operating in the United States. The company employs both Japanese nationals and U.S. nationals. You are informed by U.S. line supervisors that the Japanese workers often impede production schedules. They say the Japanese workers are overly scrupulous in observing all safety regulations, and in so doing take time away from meeting production goals. This is in contrast, the supervisors say, to the U.S. workers, who get the work out on time or ahead of schedule but who take only minimal safety precautions. The U.S. line supervisors believe that you should provide professional counseling to the Japanese workers to help them solve this problem. Discuss the various approaches that could be taken. Such approaches might include counseling the Japanese workers to concentrate more on production and to emulate their American counterparts; counseling the Americans to place more emphasis on safety and emulate their Japanese counterparts; asking the training department to institute a regular training program to insure that safety regulations be adhered to without impeding production; or looking into the cultural and behavioral factors that produce different work styles.

Discussion Question # 2

You are a career development counselor attached to an engineering project. This project team is comprised of engineers who are U.S.–born Americans and naturalized Americans from the Middle East.

At project team meetings, the U.S.–born American engineers are quick to speak up, address the issue directly, and provide immediately applicable solutions. On the other hand, the naturalized American engineers are slow to speak up and often do so only after the issue has already been resolved, address the issue from a multiplicity of viewpoints, and suggest further study or indirect solutions to the issues.

The project manager has asked you to work with the naturalized engineers about their hesitation in speaking out. In doing this you have compared their rambling discussions to the direct responses of their U.S.–born counterparts and informed them that in the United States, quick practical solutions are valued. The result of this has been that, now, they do not speak out at all! Discuss some of the possible cultural and behavioral factors that could be the cause of their behavior. Could it be because that in their culture one does not call attention to one's self by speaking out in a group or because one shows one's expertise by addressing all of the ramifications of an issue and not just the apparent problem? Maybe further study is the preferred approach in a culture where indirect solutions developed by a group are those most readily applied. Or perhaps it's due to a basic lack of education or experience in group problem solving or a discomfort in speaking in a second language.

As the career development counselor for this engineering team, discuss some of the possible approaches and solutions.

Discussion Question # 3

You are a career development professional teaching a class on successful interviewing techniques. In your class is a white male, an Afro-American male, an Afro-American female, an American-born Chinese female, a European male immigrant, and three Asian immigrants (two female and one male) from different countries in Asia. What teaching techniques would you use or not use with this group and why?

How would you help this group to prepare for corporate America?

Other Questions

▶ How could you plan an orientation program for a group of new employees of differing ethnicities and cultures?

▶ How could you develop a cross-cultural mentoring system within your corporation?

▶ How could you contribute to succession planning for those of differing cultures in your organization?

7

• • • • • • • •

Working Couples:
Finding a Balance Between Family and Career

MARK GUTERMAN

It's Sunday night about 9:00 P.M. and the couple has just finished putting their daughter, Lynn, to bed.

Partner 1: Where did the weekend go?

Partner 2: Well, between the chores, the shopping, playing with Lynn, exercising, and going out last night, it just went! It wasn't long enough for me either. So let's get on with our calendars for next week.

Partner 1: I'm already exhausted just thinking about it, and I know we have some potential scheduling conflicts. Here's my schedule: Monday—take Lynn to gym after work; Tuesday and Wednesday— work only; Thursday—school after work until 10:00 P.M; and Friday— leave work at noon to fly to Southern California for that weekend convention. I'll be home Monday night in time to go to my meeting.

Partner 2: I work both Monday and Tuesday into the evening—Monday I should be home by 10:00 and Tuesday by 8:30. Wednesday I take Lynn to gym after my short work day. Thursday and Friday are short days for me, too, so I'll pick Lynn up at the sitter. Saturday is the cat's vet appointment, Lynn's party (which means going out Friday night to buy a birthday present), and her dance lesson in the afternoon; plus there's the groceries, the yard work, and the bills. On Sunday, I'm going to a concert and then can play the rest of the day. I was supposed to travel to Kansas City this week, but had to turn it down because of our schedule and your travel. I hope that doesn't happen too often.

Partner 1: Well, you know I'm traveling again next month and have planned another weekend to visit some friends.

Partner 2: And next week, my brother is coming to visit for three days...

Partner 1: Enough already—all this on top of the routine and daily activities is more than I can think about right now! I used to love surprises, but I don't know how I could handle one more thing in my life.

Partner 2: I know what you mean! It's no wonder the time seems to fly by so fast. With so much to do and so much to take care of there's no time to be bored, do nothing, or be surprised! Sometimes I wonder if it's worth it.

Does this sound familiar? This couple's transcript is a real and ongoing dialogue in the lives of millions of working couples. In trying to get through their days, weeks, and months, time rolls on, often accompanied by the stress, anxiety, and guilt of trying to do more and more in the same 24-hour day. All aspects of their lives are affected, including the quality of their work and family life. In having such a full life, whether chosen or dictated by circumstances, there is often no time or energy left to focus on the feelings or tasks at hand. And in such a full life, how do working couples juggle their activities to find a balance between work and family?

This chapter will explore the issue of finding a balance between family and career for individuals and couples, the organizations they work in, and the counselors who assist them. It will address the career needs of working couples within the context of their families and relationships and suggest ways for couples to clarify, articulate, and communicate their needs so that they can find an optimal balance between their career and their family. It will also focus on the impact of working couples on organizational life and will conclude with ideas and information for counselors who help working couples.

Working Couples in a Changing Workplace

Before addressing specific issues, it is important to understand who and what a working couple is. Sekaran (1986) defines a dual-career couple/

family as a married couple in which both partners are involved in career-oriented work, accompanied by children and home responsibilities. Given the social and economic realities of modern times, however, the definition needs to be broadened to reflect other ways that people live together. It must also include homosexual relationships. Furthermore, the definition must also encompass both dual-career and dual-earner couples, recognizing that the latter, while not as visible, is closer to the norm than current literature would have us believe. In light of these considerations, the following definition will be used in this chapter: A working couple consists of any two people in an ongoing, committed relationship, where both partners work, where there may or may not be children, and where decisions (family and work) are influenced by the working situation of each partner.

The working couple is the dominant family arrangement in our society, but only recently has this become acknowledged. The myth of the Cleavers, the Andersons, or the Bunkers is still alive, yet the reality is that less than one family in ten fits the old model (Sekaran, 1986). And though many may wish for it, the traditional arrangement of a father working outside the home and a mother at home whose primary role and responsibility is homemaking and child care almost certainly will not be that way again.

The difficulty created by this myth and the desire by some to live in the past is that our major cultural norms and rules are still governing choices. The reality of a changed lifestyle indicates the need for new norms and rules, but it appears that the culture hasn't changed enough to meet the daily needs of working couples. And although there has been a rapid and dramatic shift of cultural norms, the workplace and support mechanisms have not kept pace with the changing needs of these families.

To complicate matters, today's working couples, who are often well-educated and have come of age with an entitlement mind-set, have high and often unrealistic expectations of actualizing their potential. These expectations cover the various roles as partners, lovers, parents, workers, and friends. Learning to clarify, communicate, and perhaps redefine expectations and values in their various roles are the central tasks facing the daily lives of working couples.

The rules have changed quickly, and few real guidelines exist for today's couples. They are making up the rules as they go along. Some key questions that once had fairly clear-cut answers are being reexamined:

▶ Whose career is more important when a promotion or new job involves relocation?

▶ If both partners must travel as part of their work, who stays home if a child becomes ill?

▶ If both partners have demanding jobs, how do they decide when family time becomes important enough to say no to work?

These are just a few of the difficult questions being asked, and because of the complexities of working couples' lives and the lack of rules for negotiating these issues, the answers don't come easily or without a great deal of stress and anxiety.

The workplace is also undergoing a profound transformation. As the lengthening workweek for managers and professionals indicates, organizations are demanding more from their employees (O'Reilly, 1990). Families are changing and career paths in organizations are changing—not necessarily in complementary ways. This leads to another set of difficult and complex questions:

▶   I'm working 50 (or more) hours a week, but where is it leading?

▶   I work so hard that I have little time and energy to enjoy the fruits of my labor. Why?

▶   If I were to go to another company or start my own business, would my situation be any better?

▶   How do I plan for my career, given my family needs, my partner's career needs, and my organization's needs?

The last question often leads to feelings of despair, because for many it feels as if there is no way to manage so many issues at once. There is good news, however. Although we are in the midst of accelerating change, the evidence suggests that individuals, couples, and organizations are reassessing their priorities and that they are wrestling with the important questions (Ehrlich, 1989). And although organizations have been slow to change, they are beginning to respond to the needs. Programs for job-sharing, flextime and flexplace, and child care are becoming prominent, and while only a small percentage of the organizations have formalized and institutionalized these programs, the needs of working couples clearly will be a dominant theme in shaping the culture of tomorrow's workplace.

Understanding Change

While waiting for organizations to catch up with their needs, what can working couples do? What information, strategies, and methods can help them through the daily routine while meeting the needs of work and keeping in mind their long-term goals? First, it helps to recognize that whenever change is the order of the day, as it most certainly will be for the foreseeable future, an understanding of the change process is essential. Because all change is accompanied by stress and anxiety, the current rapid pace brings enormous difficulties and a strong desire from many to avoid, deny, stop, or turn back to simpler times. And although any of these alternatives may solve short-term problems, they usually are not the most effective ways to manage busy lives and demanding workplaces.

All change involves loss. Most people and organizations try to avoid loss and the associated feelings. The partners in a working couple must face up to changing roles, changing rules, and changing relationships and begin to accept that these changes are not easy and can be avoided only for so long and only at a price. By understanding both individual and organizational change processes and our reactions to them, individuals can begin to develop alternative and more positive ways to manage change. When one begins to realize that the rules, roles, and relationships have forever been altered, only then can one look hopefully and openly to a future where flexibility, trust, and openness will be required as survival skills in a world of ambiguity and complexity. Flexibility will enable people to adapt to new situations quickly and easily and with less stress. Trusting oneself and one's partner will give people a sense of power and purpose as they move into the future. And an openness to one's feelings and experiences will help people find guidance and direction from the inside when everything around them is changing so fast.

Issues for Working Couples

In accepting and embracing the process of change as an integral part of life, what can working couples do to find a balance between family and career? Of primary significance, couples need to consider where they are now, where they want to go, and how they will get there. Since these involve both the "we" and "I," conflicts and differences in priority and timing will undoubtedly arise, some of which may be difficult to work through. As a result, the first requirement is open and honest communication.

Communication

Recent literature shows that partners spend little time in quality communication, that is, in intimate conversation or working out problems together, except when one or both are in crisis (Levine, 1988). At that point it is often too late to solve the real problem, and a breakup of a relationship or an unwise job change can result.

Think of the last time you had quality communication with your partner. When was it? What was the focus? Were you really there for your partner, able to listen and support, and was your partner able to do the same for you? Many couples cannot remember the last time they had this kind of encounter with their partners, and although they recognize the importance of it, they are often too busy and too tired to make it happen. Communication is so important that couples should plan regularly scheduled times for communication (and not just to review weekly calendars as the couple at the beginning of the chapter did). The frequency is less important than a sincere effort to talk about the key questions noted above.

The first consideration—for couples to assess where they are—is usually the most difficult and also the most important. Often when a couple finally sits down for this kind of communication, they are so out of practice, so fearful, or so preoccupied that they don't know where to begin. Because there may be so much that has not been said, it is important that each partner communicate honestly and clearly what is going on for them. A simple and effective exercise to get the communication started is to have one partner pose three statements to the other:

▶ Tell me something about yourself.

▶ Tell me something about me.

▶ Tell me something about our relationship.

The other partner should not speak or interrupt until the first is finished. Then they can respond and give feedback. Once completed the roles are reversed. This breaks the ice and can set the tone for constructive and positive communication sessions.

Priorities

Once the communication begins, a helpful exercise that couples can practice is called the Pie of Life, based on the assumption that people's priorities are reflected in how they spend their time. Each person (older children can also participate in this exercise) draws a circle on a piece of paper and then segments the circle according to how much time is spent on various activities (e. g., work, child care, sleep, leisure activities, couple time, meals, study/school, etc.) in a typical day or week. This gives each person a picture of where they are and provides the basis for looking at what's working and what's not. Before discussing these issues with the partner, a second pie can be drawn to describe how the partner's day or week is perceived. These two drawings provide the basis for a discussion of oneself and perceptions of the partner. In looking at and discussing how time is spent, partners can quickly get a feel for where each is and from there can begin to move on to discuss different perceptions and conflicts that face one another.

For example, an automobile assembler who worked the swing shift was married to a secretary whose hours were nine to five. They found themselves in the midst of great conflict and stress and were at a loss as to what to do. The Pie of Life showed them quickly and graphically how their perceptions of one another were inaccurate and were leading each to assume the worst about the other. After several sessions using data from their exercises, they began to come to a common ground, particularly in the areas of child care and managing the house. Eventually, the auto worker moved to a day-shift job, at slightly less money, to help his partner with the house and children.

Roles

The roles played by family members are another critical area for working couples to examine and discuss. These roles will be as diverse as there are families, but it is important to know what they are, who is playing them, and how they are working to support that person and the well-being of the family. As roles become identified and clarified, the pathway for negotiating, compromising, and reassigning becomes clearer. Eventually members of families can work toward roles that suit not only their individual needs but those of the family as well.

As a way to identify roles and open the discussion toward a more flexible role orientation, the following exercise can be helpful. On the left-hand side of a sheet of paper, the partners can make a list of all the roles that occur in the family (this can be one list generated by the couple together). These may include provider, nurturer, fix-it person, babysitter, meal-preparer, chaperone, chauffeur, bill-payer, dreamer, TV-watcher, and so on. After this list is completed, each partner, on their own, notes who plays which roles, and if there are split roles, the approximate weighting in the split. Once completed, each partner exchanges his or her list with the other. Issues to be discussed may include differences in perception, roles played willingly and consciously, roles that no one likes but need doing for family survival, and so on. After agreement is reached on the roles and who takes them on, the next part is to figure out what changes, if any, need to be made (e.g., rotation of responsibilities, leave of absence from work, delegation of chores, lowering standards in agreed upon areas, paying someone else to take on certain roles, etc.) and how each sees his or her respective roles as contributing to or hindering the well-being of the family.

This exercise was used with a working couple where one partner, whose income was more than double his partner's, began to resent being the main provider and watching his partner's larger spending role. The partner, who also had a demanding although much lower-paying job, and who was the primary homemaker, became angry at her partner's lack of emotional support and understanding of her needs. She did not feel that her contributions were valued as much as his. As they identified their various roles and discussed their resentments and fears, they began to make decisions about how to do things differently. Among other things, the higher-income partner began to pay for services of outsiders (e.g., a gardener and a housekeeper), which greatly diminished the pressure on the homemaker.

The thrust of the exercises so far have placed work and career in the context of the family, but because work commands so much time and energy and may dictate many or most of the roles for some couples, other specific questions need to be asked and discussed:

▶ If work takes up a significant portion of a person's time and energy, is there enough left for other important tasks and roles?

▶ If the answer is yes, does the partner agree?

▶ If the answer is no, what does each person intend to do about it?

Many people have sufficient nonwork time, but are so consumed by their work that they are not fully present during nonworking hours.

▶ How do partners feel about the quality of attention they receive during nonwork hours?

▶ If there are children, how do they feel about the attention they receive from parents?

▶ As the partners look at the balance between family and career, are they satisfied?

Whether satisfied or not, the next set of broad considerations needs to be addressed: Where do they go from here and how do they get there?

Values

Before moving ahead, however, the values of a couple must be considered if counselors are to be effective in helping them find balance in their lives. Articulating and clarifying values can help people discover what matters most to them and why they might be happy or unhappy with their current situation; it also forms the basis for setting future directions. This process is important because it establishes compatibility between individual values and career choices and also because it forms a foundation for partners to communicate to each other what is most important to them.

When thinking and speaking of values, those that relate to work and career—challenge, growth, opportunity, security, money, recognition, prestige, and power—are only part of the picture. Deeply held life values must also be articulated, explored, and communicated. These can include contributing to society, pursuing hobbies and leisure activities, practicing spiritual or religious beliefs, continuing to learn, spending time with the family, and so on. Identifying these values—both work values and broader life values—takes time and effort. Asking the partner what he or she sees as the other's values is an important and necessary exercise if effective decisions are to be made. And because it may take time and energy to uncover and articulate what these values are, it is important to ask the question, What is most important to me and us? on a regular and frequent basis.

In another example, one member of a couple had the opportunity for a challenging and exciting job in another geographic location. Her partner, whose life and career were clearly connected to the current location, at first simply refused to hear of a probable relocation. After several sessions where shared values were explored, they began to identify what was most important to both of them. She wanted risks and challenges, while he valued security. It was agreed that the relocating partner would move for a trial period of three months. If the new job worked out (which was to be jointly discussed and agreed on), the settled partner would then make plans to move to the new location. While not an ideal solution for either one, they both felt this was the closest they could get to satisfying their shared values.

There are, of course, many other ways for couples to discover where they are now, and as the questions continue to be asked, other ways will emerge. What is most important is that both partners be willing to engage themselves and each other in the questioning process and be ready and willing to hear each other's answers. There will no doubt be differences and conflicts, some of which may be relatively easy to resolve and some much more difficult. The clearer people are about the roles, values, and tasks, and the more willing they are to communicate those to each other, the more likely the couple will be able to establish meaningful goals for themselves, their family, and their career.

Managing Daily Life

Once the couple has a sense of the current situation, they need to consider how they are doing day to day and how they can do it more effectively. Once resolved, they need to focus on the future, identifying for each other their goals and dreams. How do they talk about them together? How do they make the necessary choices and trade-offs that will get them both what they want from family and career?

In managing their daily lives, working couples often experience overload, guilt, stress, and anxiety as they try to cram into 24 hours all the activities that have become part of their lives. One of the key variables for the successful working couple is flexibility in both roles and tasks.

Although the working couple is becoming the dominant family arrange-ment, roles in many of these families are still tradition bound (Hochschild, 1989). Those couples who are most successful in balancing family and career are those who have redefined the various roles of each partner in such a way that both partners are equally capable of doing what needs to be done to keep the family moving on a day-to-day basis.

This means that each partner needs to not only let go of their often high and unrealistic expectations of themselves but also to be willing to support and acknowledge their partner for learning new and necessary behaviors and skills. Each partner will undoubtedly maintain preferences and dislikes, but couples need to remember that roles must be fluid between the partners and each person must remain committed to the accomplishment of the family's work.

This extends beyond household or parenting responsibilities. Tradi-tionally, it was one partner who always stayed home with the sick child or who acted as chauffeur and overseer, and thereby did not or could not put as much energy into a career. As roles change, definitions of success change. As definitions of success change, partners in working couples are beginning to realize that both must be willing to give to the family, and both may have to give up something in return. These changes usually create stress and confusion, and working couples often struggle to walk a fine line between changing definitions of career success and the changing nature of roles at home.

Part of the difficulty stems from having no role models and no clear guidelines or definitions of "how it ought to be." Caught between their individual and family needs and a social system and workplace that is not yet fully responsive, working couples are making up the rules as they go along. They often rely on their instincts or support from peers who are in similar circumstances, both of which are important but usually not sufficient to deal with all the issues. Sometimes they reach out to parents, mentors, and elders, who may consequently have difficulty understanding the pressures and issues and offer advice that only confuses the couple.

Managing Stress

One result of these changes and new roles is a growing level of stress. Even as we are learning more about the causes, results, and management of stress, stress for working couples continues to grow. They are often so tired that they willingly forego sex. Their two, three, or even four weeks of vacation each year are not enough to replenish their energy. They become obsessed with staying fit to the point where it becomes just another source of stress. This growing stress is widely recognized, and there is alarm in some areas that the long-range health effects of such stress could be devastating (Cavanagh, 1988). Yet many couples deny, ignore, or postpone dealing with the stress issue, even though they may be aware of the harm in doing so.

Effective strategies can be taken, however. Managing stress is more than learning to relax, although a regular regimen of relaxation and exercise is far superior to doing nothing. Effective stress management looks for ways to reduce sources of stress, examines how one reacts and responds to stress, and includes a regular practice of stress-reducing methods. In addition to the sources of stress already mentioned, it is fairly clear that organizations are expecting more from their employees, such as longer hours and improved productivity. Thus, at the same time a couple is trying to juggle changing roles and responsibilities, their workplaces are demanding more from them. Some workplaces offer flexible working arrangements and stress management courses, but these are the exception. Flexible arrangements are often available only to those employees who have the clout and/or savvy to negotiate for it.

While many organizations are changing, the direction and pace of the change often work against a lower stress environment, especially on a day-to-day basis, where it has immediate impact on people's well-being. In spite of this, employees can take responsibility to assert their needs for a moderated stress environment within the context of larger family needs. Many employees are afraid to speak up for fear of losing jobs and promotions, but if employees do not assert their needs, organizations will continue to demand more in their drive to improve productivity. And if organizations do not respond to these pressing and immediate needs, then employees may need to seek action through legislation that will promote a better balance between family and career.

Even as the workplace continues to change, partners in working couples must take responsibility for managing their own stress. This includes examining one's attitudes and practicing a regimen of stress-reduction techniques. One set of attitudes stems from the values process described earlier in this chapter. If a person's values are centered around power, accomplishment, and traditional success, then the price paid to achieve those may lead to chronic and long-term stress. So as values are being defined, clarified, and communicated, it becomes important to ask, How will my valuing this help or hinder my physical and mental well-being? All of the perks associated with power and success will amount to little if the person is too sick, tired, or burned out to enjoy them.

Another set of attitudes that must be examined are those developed toward stressors in the environment. Adams (1980) states that stress can either be positive or negative, and often it is our attitude that determines which it will be. Some people are able to relax in the heat of crisis, and others get frazzled over the smallest details. It is important to examine one's attitudinal response to stressful events and to reexamine those attitudes that are continually setting one up to view situations as negative, worrisome, or anxiety-provoking.

Even positive stress, however, can take its toll on the body, and any kind of stress, if maintained for too long a period at too much intensity, will begin to cause breakdowns for people. Most working couples recognize how busy and often overly planned their lives are. While they may be doing what they enjoy and care about, the stress level may be reaching dangerous proportions. This pace and stress get translated to the children, whose own schedules may resemble those of the busiest executives. In their need to achieve and succeed, working couples are placing their children under enormous pressure and at a time when the children are the most vulnerable and least equipped to cope. Some school districts are now offering courses to teach parents how to notice stress in their preschool children.

The last component of stress management is the practice of a stress reduction routine. Given that organizations and lifestyles will not change significantly in the short term, it becomes important to know and practice preventive measures for stress management. Most of the techniques are simple to do and inexpensive to learn, can be done privately and at home, and do not require elaborate equipment or time commitments. On the other hand, many people are simply too busy to bring another routine into their lives, no matter how beneficial it may seem. Rather than letting something go, the relaxation practice or the jogging becomes another thing that needs to be done in an already overly full schedule. Under these circumstances, a stress reduction practice, or the guilt when not accomplished, may actually increase that person's stress level.

The Response in the Workplace

So where does the organization fit into this picture, and how do our workplaces support or hinder a couple's capacity for balancing family and career? Organizations are facing more pressure than ever before to come halfway in meeting the needs of working couples (Conference Board, 1988).

Flexibility

Earlier, before the onset of the global marketplace and the instant information age, an organization's primary struggle was to maximize profits in a growing and unlimited arena. Today organizations are fighting for their survival in what looks and feels like a shrinking marketplace. Because these pressures are real and enormous, decision makers in organizations are

faced with keeping costs down and driving productivity up. This sometimes means that although the organization may speak of the importance
of their human resources, most organizations see people as a significant
cost of doing business, a cost that must be kept under control and at a
minimum.

At the same time that organizations are feeling the need to keep tighter
controls on expenses and costs, individuals and couples have a growing
need for a more flexible and open workplace. This paradox is frustrating
both employees and organizations, and few have learned how to manage
both sides of the dilemma. Of course, there are many progressive
organizations and workplaces, but the majority of working couples are
adapting to the needs of the organization rather than the other way around.
The stories of flextime, job-sharing, and working at home through
computers, while encouraging, are still the exception, and the flexibility
needed by most working couples in their organizations is not yet a reality.

Organizations are finding it increasingly difficult to recruit the talented
employees they need to be successful. This is partly because of a shortage
of skilled employees and partly due to the fact that the needs of working
couples are not being adequately met by the employers. Many organizations are still trying to attract employees with promises of promotions,
advancement, and the like, yet because of continual restructuring in many
organizations, rapid promotions for most employees will not happen and
advancement upward to the top may become a myth for this generation
of workers (Bardwick, 1986). Add to that the need of many organizations
to relocate and move people to meet their business needs, and the reality
of organizational life no longer matches the needs and values of many
working couples.

Cafeteria Benefits

As organizations find it more difficult to recruit and retain valued
employees, many are beginning to respond to the needs of working
couples. One of the most obvious and widely accepted benefits for
working couples is the cafeteria or flexible benefits plan, in which a set
dollar amount for each employee is provided from which to select the types
and levels of benefits most suitable to their needs. This is a benefit when
both working partners have a redundancy in the types of coverage offered
by their employers. Some organizations are now including dollars for child
care expenses as well. A large clothing manufacturer is looking at ways to
offer employees a core benefits package supplemented by flex components
(including child care reimbursement) to make up a complete benefits
program. This helps working couples put together a benefits program that
serves their needs as employees, partners, and parents.

Child Care

Child care has become a significant issue in the workplace. A growing number of organizations, prodded by their employees and possible legislation, are providing some support for child care (Sandroff, 1989). And those that do are aware of the number of current and potential employees who list the availability of child care as one of their key criteria for taking a job with a new organization. Most of the organizations that are active in this area provide little more than information and referral services, but more and more are providing on-site, near-site, or subsidized child care or making provisions that benefit dollars be used to pay for child care. A public utilities firm in the Southwest has begun providing an information and referral service in addition to offering a fixed dollar amount for employees to use for child care (or to be used to buy other benefits if child care is not needed). And a West Coast biotechnology company has found its on-site child care center to be valuable in attracting and retaining the talent it needs to stay at the top of its field. Since adequate and affordable child care is a necessity for so many people today, those organizations that hope to attract the best employees will eventually see that the benefits of supporting child care far outweigh the costs. If organizations don't act, the legislative process will at some point force them into solutions that may or may not be in their best interests.

Relocation and Recruitment

A larger number of organizations are beginning to provide assistance for partners of employees who are asked to relocate (Collie, 1989). Many employees will no longer consider a move, even for a significant promotion, unless some sort of assistance is provided for their partner. Because so many couples value and depend on each other's career, either one is likely to hesitate and think very carefully about the ramifications of a relocation on the partner and the relationship. Since most organizations have no real interest or expertise in providing career counseling or job search assistance to partners, those that see a need are beginning to contract with career agencies in the new location to help the partner find new employment. For example, a multistate construction and design firm now offers career and job search assistance to partners of relocating employees. Another alternative is to provide the partner with a fixed dollar amount, and the partner than takes responsibility for seeking his or her own reemployment assistance.

Whatever stance the organization takes, there is a growing recognition that these newer lifestyle arrangements call for new and innovative recruiting techniques. Because many employees are making career decisions based on what is best for them as well as for their partner and family, organizations are being forced into areas where they have little knowledge and comfort. There is much resistance and resentment on the part of organizations, and many are either ignoring the needs or reluctantly developing what to them appear to be frivolous and costly programs that have only a negative impact on their bottom line. What they still do not see clearly is that without these kinds of efforts, they will find it increasingly difficult to attract and retain valuable and skilled employees. But as more members of working couples become the decision makers in their organizations, this resistance will fade and be replaced by new ways of looking at costs and benefits that factor these realities into profit and growth formulas.

Productivity

Keeping employees productive is another challenge faced by organizations. As working couples comprise an increasing portion of the work force, organizations find themselves competing for their time, energy, and attention. Because many working couples have children and even aging parents to care for, they often come to work with much on their minds that has nothing to do with work. Often these other responsibilities result in greater absenteeism and tardiness, more personal phone calls, and less attention paid to work projects. Organizations cannot stop people from taking care of necessities, and many are taking steps to minimize the impact through a variety of methods.

One of the most prevalent ways to keep employee productivity up is the use of flextime. Recognizing that the needs of working partners and parents do not always correspond precisely to business hours, many organizations offer formal and informal ways for employees to flex their time schedules. As long as the work is getting done, more organizations are moving to the flextime concept (Olmsted & Smith, 1989). This has been expanded to include the concept of flexplace, where many employees do a good portion of their work at home through use of computers and fax machines. The civilian division of a metropolitan police department offers employees several work options, including nine days of work in a two-week period or four days of work in a one-week period. They have also started a pilot program in their systems division to explore *telecommuting,* using personal computers, modems, and fax machines, for example, from an outside location to do their work. The early fears that people would not work as hard away from the workplace have proved unfounded, and in most cases, people's productivity and satisfaction improve measurably when they are given the opportunity to work at home (Hamilton, 1987).

Other variations that organizations are using to meet the needs of working couples while maintaining productivity include job-sharing, part-time managerial and professional positions, and temporary or contract work (Bergsman, 1989). Organizations are not necessarily happy about or supportive of these new arrangements, but those that do not work to meet the family needs of their employees will find it increasingly difficult to recruit and retain the needed talent to be successful. A computer manufacturer, while reluctant to develop a formal policy, says that many individual employees and their managers are devising alternate work arrangements, especially for the first year after a child is born. A Midwest chemical manufacturer offers paid parental leave, guarantees a job and adjustable hours upon return, and allows employees to use sick leave to care for an ill child or parent. Those organizations that have changed have found mostly positive results. While administrative headaches often accompany alternative work arrangements, most organizations have found that the benefits in increased productivity and improved morale have significantly outweighed the costs.

Recognizing that employees are under tremendous pressure from both the workplace and their life situations, many organizations are beginning to actively support stress management programs for their employees. These may consist of stress reduction workshops, mental health days off from work, and parental leave for care of newborn or sick children. Some organizations have space available on-site where employees can spend some quiet time. Others are beginning to follow the academic model by offering lengthy sabbaticals for employees with several years of continuous service (Rubin, 1987).

Career Pathing and Mobility

Career paths and mobility are also undergoing change. As hierarchies flatten and as individual and couple needs enter into the career pathing formula, organizations are slowly and reluctantly redefining traditional definitions of career success. It is clear that organizations will continue to need talented people to ascend to positions of authority, but that road continues to grow longer and much more inaccessible to most workers. If organizations are to keep and motivate the necessary human resources, they need to recognize and acknowledge that not all employees will be on the fast track. New programs that offer reward and development for those who cannot or will not commit as much time and energy must be provided if organizations are to keep their best people. As more people choose to work less than full-time, or with breaks (for child or elder care, sabbatical, etc.), or from home, career paths will be redefined to such an extent that traditional career ladders will be a thing of the past.

The key to an organization's success and future is arguably how they manage their human resources, which grows increasingly more complex everyday. Managers and decision makers must examine the needs of their organization in light of changing values and newer lifestyles and build their businesses accordingly. This means that managers must become sensitive to the needs of the changing work force and understand how these needs impact their business. Managers must educate themselves and take a leadership role in helping their organizations and their employees adapt to a changing world. As a starting place, these new realities and their potential impact should become an integral part of the organization's mission statement and profit/growth formulas. This requires an openness and flexibility on the part of managers and a willingness to see that their people are a critical link in their survival and success.

Organizations and their managers—many of whom are partners in a working couple—are responding slowly and reluctantly in the face of rapid social and cultural change. Those who will not or cannot adapt will find it increasingly difficult to maintain an effective organization. They will be staffed by less talented employees and hurt by their inflexibility as much in the marketplace as in managing their human resources. If they survive, they will be the mediocre organizations of the future. Those who are able to adapt, whether willingly or grudgingly, will find themselves with a loyal and productive work force. This also means that organizations will have to bring their human resource processes and their strategic process into closer synchronization, and while that is undoubtedly difficult, it will be rewarded handsomely in productivity, market share, and profitability. These organizations will not only succeed, they will also be the model organizations of the future—organizations with that rare blend of business savvy combined with real care and concern for their employees.

New Roles for the Career Counselor

Career counselors play a vital role as a link between the individual/couple and the organization. Whether working in an organization or outside, career counselors are uniquely positioned to assist in understanding the needs and issues of working couples and developing programs and processes to benefit both the organization and the individual. To do this effectively, career counselors must look at the roles they play now and how those might change to help working couples find a balance between family and career.

Broadening the Concept of Career Decision Making

In examining their role in counseling individuals, it is clear that career counseling must consider a broader context than in the past. Whether working with individuals or with groups, career counselors need to offer interventions, exercises, and questions that will assist their clients to broaden the context of their career decisions. These might include asking how the client's decision will influence the partner's career and how the decision will affect the whole family. The counselor may want to have clients broaden their values clarification by looking at the compatibility between their own values and the values of their partner and examining how both sets of values play into individual career choice and family issues.

The career counselor can then help the client to articulate the various dilemmas that may arise. For example, when partners are trying to make a decision about whether and when to have children, the counselor can assist them in setting their career priorities within a family context and help them to sequence their decisions over time so they do not feel that everything has to happen at once. Career counselors can help clients select occupations and careers that are compatible with the lifestyle choices that are important to them.

Couples Counseling

From the counselor's point of view, it might make sense to meet with both partners so that the career decision-making process can be seen in the context of the relationship. Because it is difficult for career counselors to know how their interventions will be received by a partner or family, the career counselor who works with both partners can get a more complete picture of what the client may be facing in making a decision. This can also help partners improve their communication skills, which may serve to benefit other areas of their lives.

It may be that career counselors will eventually teach their clients and partners additional skills beyond career planning, career decision making, or job search strategies. These might include communication skills, conflict resolution and negotiation skills, time management, and stress management skills. In addition, career counselors who choose to work with couples will find themselves dealing with individual and couple issues of guilt, power, alienation, competition, anger, and other factors, which may take the career counselor into new and perhaps uncomfortable territory. One thought would be to team up with psychotherapists to do conjoint career counseling for couples and families.

Career counselors need to encourage their clients to let go of past models and take risks to create new roles and rules. The process can encourage an exploration of the "shoulds" (i.e., the man should provide, the woman should nurture, etc.) and of myths held by clients. Together they can work toward replacing those myths with appropriate roles for their own careers and families. Helping clients move toward role redefinition and role flexibility is difficult and tedious, and this can be facilitated greatly if counselors are moving toward this in their own life. In moving toward a balance between their own families and careers, career counselors can be models for their clients and have more empathy for their needs.

Organizational Influence

Career counselors in organizations will increasingly find themselves assisting clients to focus on broader questions than simply, What's available to me in this organization and how do I get there? They will also be in a position to advise the organization on career-family interaction and how this affects the performance and productivity of employees. As organizations continue to change, career counselors can serve as important links in providing valuable information to the organizational decision makers and can communicate organizational trends and realities to employees.

More specifically, organizational career development programs will become more closely aligned with other development processes in the organization. Employee assistance programs, for example, will call on career development to help their clients deal more ably with stresses that hinder their work performance. Management development programs will call on career counselors to offer training, workshops, and consultation in the area of how managers can sensitize themselves to the needs of working couples, including managerial strategies for motivation and reward. The organization development function will need to know more about individual career concerns if they are to design and deliver effective team-building programs. And succession planners will need to be sensitized to and plan for key individuals' life goals when they put together vital succession plans for the organization.

In addition to the specific functions, the career counselor can play an important role in helping the organization to recognize the values and needs of a changing work force. By communicating individual needs for flexible working arrangements and other progressive programs to help working couples, and by helping the organization to understand these needs as legitimate for both individual and organizational success, the career counselor becomes an advocate for needed change in many organizations. In working with employees and their career and family issues, the career counselor can use that information to recommend and propose programs designed to meet both individual and organizational needs.

Counselors as Advocates for Social Change

Career counselors are playing a growing role in our society, whether working with individuals, couples, or organizations. The processes of career and job change, including goal setting, planning, and job-search strategies, grow increasingly more important as society becomes more complex. Career counselors are in a position to articulate these needs, not only for individuals in transition or for organizations in need of people, but also for the larger society. Career counselors hear everyday the needs of working couples, and whether through writing or speaking or being an advocate for child care legislation, they are in a position to be key spokespersons for helping to achieve a balance between family and career.

As a critical part of this advocacy, career counselors can also begin to help individuals and society redefine career success. Past definitions of success, including climbing the corporate ladder and amassing power and money, no longer hold the same meaning or allure for many working couples. Instead, they are beginning to define success in broader terms that include such things as time with family, sense of community, time for relationships, and being a part of their children's development. Career counselors can be an important influence in helping to redefine success as a balancing of family and career and then helping their clients move toward finding that balance.

Continuing Education for Counselors

As a result of these emerging roles, career counselors must continue to enhance their own knowledge, skills, and abilities. As more working couples seek career counseling, either as individuals or as partners, career counselors will need a thorough understanding of couple and family dynamics. They will also need to be well versed in adult development concepts and will begin to apply both in creating and using interventions that recognize the complexity in counseling working couples.

Career counselors will also need more knowledge of organizational dynamics and development. As organizations continue to go through profound change, counselors will benefit from an understanding of basic business concepts, organizational life cycles, and human resource concepts and practices and how these can alter a client's career decision as part of a working couple. Many career counselors have limited exposure and experience in business, and since most of their clients will work in some form of business setting, counselors must have more grounding in business issues. Business courses, internships, short term or part-time jobs, information gathering interviews, and continuous study of business trends must be a part of the career counselor's development plans.

Because we live in an age of continuous change, career counselors need to be willing to engage the change process themselves. This means not only a thorough understanding of transition and change issues, but also a willingness to change themselves. Career counselors unwilling to try new jobs, new ways of working, and even switching careers will eventually lose credibility with their clients who are changing and will invariably be out of touch with the workplaces they are recommending to their clients. Career counselors need to be continuously learning and taking risks in order to be effective at teaching the process of career planning and career change to their clients.

Conclusion

All the players in the career drama are facing dilemma, stress, and confusion as well as excitement, change, and opportunity. For the partner in a working couple, choices must take into account such variables as availability of child care, if and when to have children, the importance of the partner's career, and so on. Organizations, increasingly focused on a competitive marketplace, must pay attention to the growing impact of working couples, both as employees and as potential business. And career counselors who assist organizations and individuals to link their wants and needs must know more about each side of the equation to be effective in their work.

The decisions are growing more complex, and the ambiguity caused by changing norms and rules creates added stress. More and more people are talking about slowing down and not being as consumed by career and ambition. More and more people are choosing to work in ways that are compatible with other needs in their lives. More and more people are speaking of trade-offs and seeking to find some kind of balance in their lives. More and more organizations are accommodating the needs of their employees and working couples. It is a time of change, and although it is not going as smoothly or as quickly as some would like, the indications are that working couples are making a positive and profound impact on our society.

At a recent presentation on "Issues for Working Couples" (Guterman, 1989) delivered to a group of psychotherapists and employee assistance providers, the audience asked, "Is there any hope?" The speaker paused for a moment and then responded,

> Yes, there is reason for hope, but each of us here and in our organizations must take the risk to know and communicate what is important to us. Change will feel slow for those whose daily lives are harried and busy, but change will come if we remain patient, persistent, and not get too caught up in the daily routine. Yes, I am hopeful! Hopeful that each of us will commit to our own well-being and to the effectiveness of our organizations, and to defining those in such a way that individuals, couples and organizations come to agree that solutions that work for one must work for all.

It's Sunday night about 9:00 P.M. and Lynn is reading quietly in her bedroom. It is now 18 months later in the lives of this family.

Partner 1: The time sure does fly.

Partner 2: It sure does, and I'm really pleased with how things have been going lately.

Partner 1: So am I! Lynn is getting easier as she gets older, and I don't feel as tired as I used to.

Partner 2: And since my company restructured and I was able to negotiate working at home two days a week, I don't feel nearly as harried and rushed.

Partner 1: I also think that our talking about what we want from work and each other has really made a difference.

Partner 2: I agree. I know that for a long time I didn't understand what you were dealing with, and now that I recognize the pressures, I am more sensitive to your needs.

Partner 1: Thanks! I know, too, that I wasn't as supportive of you and all that time you spent in school. In my head I knew what you needed, but I just used to be so angry.

Partner 2: I'm just glad we worked and talked while it was happening and didn't wait.

Partner 1: Me too! I know we have a lot to do this week, so let's take a look at our calendars.

References

Adams, J. (1980). *Understanding and managing stress.* San Diego: University Associates.

Bardwick, J. (1986). *The plateauing trap: How to avoid it in your career and in your life.* New York: Amacom.

Bergsman, S. (1989). Part-time professionals make the choice. *Personnel Administrator, 34*(9), 49–52.

Cavanagh, M. (1988). What you don't know about stress. *Personnel Journal, 67*(7), 53–59.

Collie, H. C. (1989). Two salaries, one relocation: What's a company to do? *Personnel Administrator, 34*(9), 54–57.

Conference Board. (1988). *Management briefing: Human resources.* New York: Author.

Ehrlich, E. (1989, September). How the next decade will differ? *Business Week,* 142–156.

Guterman, M. (1989, November). *Issues for working couples.* ALMACA.

Hamilton, C. (1987). Telecommuting. *Personnel Journal, 66*(4), 91–101.

Hochschild, A. (1989). *The second shift: Working parents and the revolution at home.* New York: Viking.

Levine, K. (1988, June). Us time. *Parents Magazine,* 67–74.

Olmsted, B., & Smith, S. (1989). Flex for success! *Personnel, 66*(6), *50*(5).

O'Reilly, B. (1990, March). Is your company asking too much? *Fortune,* 39–46.

Rubin, B. M. (1987). *Time out.* New York: Norton.

Sandroff, R. (1989, November). Helping your company become family friendly. *Working Woman,* 136-137.

Sekaran, U. (1986). *Dual-career families.* San Francisco: Jossey Bass.

Bibliography

Ametea, E. S., & Cross, E. G. (1983). Coupling and careers: A workshop for dual career couples at the launching stage. *Personnel and Guidance Journal, 62*(1), 48–52.

Bird, C. (1975). *The two-paycheck marriage.* New York: Rawson Wade.

Conference Board. (1985). *Corporations and families: Changing practices and perspectives* (Report No. 868). New York: Author.

Friedman, D. E. (1987). Work vs. family: War of the worlds. *Personnel Administrator, 32*(7), 36–38.

Gilbert, L. A. (1985). *Men in dual career families: Current realities and future prospects.* Hillsdale, NJ: Erlbaum.

Gilbert, L. A., & Rachlin, V. (1987). Mental health and psychological functioning of dual-career families. *The Counseling Psychologist, 15*(1), 7–49.

Grieff, B. S., & Munter, P. K. (1980). *Tradeoffs: Executive, family and organizational life.* New York: Mentor.

Hall, F., & Hall, D. (1979). *The two-career couple: He works, she works, but how does the relationship work?* Reading, MA: Addison-Wesley.

Holmstrom, L. L. (1972). *The two-career family.* Cambridge, MA: Schenkman.

Hood, J. C. (1983). *Becoming a two-job family.* New York: Praeger.

Jump, T. L. (1981). *Dual career families: The interfaces of work, family and the home.* Unpublished manuscript, Indiana University, Bloomington, IN.

Kimball, G. (1983). *The 50-50 marriage.* Boston: Beacon Press.

McCroskey, J. (1982). Work and families: What is the employer's responsibility? *Personnel Journal, 61*(1), 30–38.

Miller, C. S. (1985). Dual careers: Impact on individuals, families, and organizations. In V. J. Ramsey (Ed.), *Preparing professional women for the future*. Ann Arbor: University of Michigan (Graduate School of Business Administration).

Miller, J. V. (1984). *The family-career connection: A new framework for career development* (Report No. NIE-C-400 81-0035). Columbus, OH: Ohio State University, The National Center for Research in Vocational Education. (ERIC Document Reproduction Service No. ED 246 397)

O'Neil, J. M., Mastrandrea Fishman, D., & Kinsella-Shaw, M. (1987). Dual-career couples' career transitions and normative dilemmas: A preliminary assessment. *The Counseling Psychologist, 15*(1), 50–96.

Pepitone-Rockwell, F. (Ed.). (1980). *Dual-career couples*. Beverly Hills, CA: Sage.

Pleck, J. H. (1985). *Working wives/working husbands*. Beverly Hills, CA: Sage.

Rapoport, R., & Rapoport, R. (1971). *Dual-career families*. Baltimore: Penguin Books.

Rapoport, R., & Rapoport, R. (1976). *Dual-career families re-examined*. New York: Harper Colophon Books.

Rice, D. G. (1979). *Dual career marriage, conflict and treatment*. New York: Macmillan.

Sekaran, U. (1986). *Dual career families*. San Francisco: Jossey-Bass.

Shaevitz, M., & Shaevitz, M. (1980). *Making it together as a two-career couple*. Boston: Houghton Mifflin.

Shimberg, E. F., & Beach, D. (1981). *Two for the money: A woman's guide to a double-career marriage*. Englewood Cliffs, NJ: Prentice-Hall.

Skinner, D. (1984, October). *Managing in dual-employed families: Policies and perspectives that would help*. Paper presented at the annual meeting of the National Council on Family Relations, San Francisco.

Smith, A., & Reid, W. (1986). *Role-sharing marriage*. New York: Columbia University Press.

Stautberg, S. (1987). Status report: The corporation and trends in family issues. *Human Resource Management, 26*(2), 277–290.

Stelck, L., & Newman, C. (1986). *The working relationship: Management strategies for contemporary couples*. New York: Villard Books.

Walker, L. S., Rozee-Koker, P., & Strudler Wallston, B. (1987). Social policy and the dual-career family: Bringing the social context into counseling. *The Counseling Psychologist, 15*(1), 97–121.

Wilcox-Matthew, L., & Minor, C. W. (1989). The dual career couple: Concerns, benefits, and counseling implications. *Journal of Counseling and Development, 68*, 194–198.

Questions for Counselors

Listed below are questions that can guide counselors in dealing with working couples. Whether working with one or both partners, these questions can be used to probe for more information or to provide structure and direction for the counseling process.

▶ What are your own values and needs regarding balancing family and work?

▶ How do those values and needs facilitate or hamper your counseling a member of a working couple?

▶ How is your client's career development process slowed or deterred by his or her needs to balance family and career? How do you adjust your interventions to meet these needs?

▶ How do you work differently with clients whose needs and values are influenced by being in a working couple?

▶ How do you help working couples work through their financial considerations in setting up goals and action plans?

▶ How do members of working couples communicate their values, needs, and goals to each other, and how can you assist them in this communication?

▶ How do the organizations that employ your clients meet or fail to meet their needs for balancing family and career? What can your client do about that? What can you do about that?

▶ What strategies are available to your client to seek a balance between family and career?

▶ What assessment instruments are available to counsel members of working couples, and how can they be integrated into the counseling process?

▶ What strategies will help organizations become more sensitized to the issues and needs of working couples? What role can you play?

▶ How can you assist your clients to deal with the strains, stresses, anxieties, and guilt of their everyday lives and tasks?

▶ What models, guidelines, or conceptual maps do you follow in counseling working couples?

▶ As you look into the future and see more working couples, how will you need to grow and develop yourself?

Exercises to Use With Working Couples

1. In addition to the exercises in the chapter and traditional career planning methods and tools, the following may be useful in counseling working couples:

    ▶ Either singly or together, have the couple define and articulate the "balanced life" and what that means in terms of setting goals, making plans, and moving forward together.

    ▶ Have couples develop joint goals and plans that include the following: the specific goal and/or plans, the level of priority, resources needed, time frames, level of commitment from each person affected by the goal/plan, compromises needed to reach goals and plans, anticipated areas of disagreement and conflict, and what the couple can do to work those through.

    ▶ Have couples commit to shared time, time alone, time with children (if appropriate), and so forth on a regular and scheduled basis.

    ▶ If couples are unable or unwilling to understand or empathize with the other's career and/or family needs, have them "shadow" one another for a period of time.

    ▶ As a key to positive communication, ask couples to spend time, both in session and when alone together, acknowledging and affirming one another.

    ▶ Have partners keep a journal, which they share with counselor and each other, that addresses the following: career hopes and dreams, career fears and frustrations, family needs being met and not met, support needed to meet their needs, and feelings regarding partner's issues and needs.

2. To begin the process of communication, have one partner pose three statements to the other (the other partner should not speak or interrupt until the first is finished):

    ▶ Tell me something about yourself.

    ▶ Tell me something about me.

    ▶ Tell me something about our relationship.

3. Have clients discuss the following questions:

   ▶ Where are you now?

   ▶ Where do you want to go?

   ▶ How will you get there?

4. Assuming that how people spend their time is a clear indicator of what their priorities are, have each person (older children can also participate in this exercise) draw a circle on a piece of paper and then segment the circle according to how much time is spent on various activities in a typical day or week (e.g., work, child care, sleep, leisure activities, couple time, meals, study/school, etc.). This will give each person a picture of where they are and provide the basis for looking at what's working and what's not. Then have each person draw a second circle and divide, using similar categories to depict how the partner's day or week is spent. These two drawings provide the basis for a discussion of how each person spends time and perceives how his or her partner spends time.

5. Have each partner make a list of all the roles that occur in the family, then note who plays which roles, and if there are split roles, the approximate weighting of the split. Once completed, each partner exchanges his or her list with the other. Issues to be discussed include:

   ▶ Differences in perception

   ▶ Roles played willingly and consciously

   ▶ Roles that no one likes but are required for family survival

   After there is agreement on the roles and who takes them on, the next part is to figure out what changes, if any, need to be made (e.g., rotation of responsibilities, leave of absence from work, delegation of chores, lowering standards in agreed upon areas, paying someone else to take on certain roles, etc.) and how partners see their roles as contributing to or hindering the well-being of the family.

• • • • • • • • •

About the Contributors

Introduction

Ron Visconti, M.A., is the executive director of the Community Career Education Center, a private nonprofit career development center in San Mateo, California. Visconti also serves on several Boards of Directors related to career development and employment issues, including the San Mateo County Private Industry Council and the Employer Advisory Council of San Mateo County. He is a member of the Northern California Human Resources Council and the American Society for Training and Development. Visconti received the California Career Development Association's Career Counselsor of the Year award in 1990 and is a frequent part-time instructor, lecturer, and presenter.

1 Career and Life Planning:
A Personal Gyroscope in Times of Change

Judith A. Waterman, M.A., is a nationally board certified counselsor and career counselor. As president of Judith A. Waterman Associates and managing partner of Career Management Group, she counsels individuals, works with companies on people and productivity issues, publishes, and lectures internationally. Her belief is that individual awareness is the basis for informed development, maximum contribution, and personal fulfillment—and that companies tapping into this awareness can promote better employee satisfaction and productivity.

2   Career Development for Empowerment in a Changing Work World

Dennis T. Jaffe, Ph.D., a principal in the HeartWork Group, is a clinical psychologist and organizational consultant. He is the author of twelve books, including the management best-sellers, *Take This Job and Love It!, Working With the Ones You Love,* and *Empowerment: Building a Committed Workforce.* His education in philosophy, management, and sociology at Yale University brings a unique perspective to business challenges. He is director of the Organizational Inquiry doctoral interest area at Saybrook Institute, San Francisco. In addition, he is a nationally recognized leader in executive team development.

Cynthia D. Scott, Ph.D., M.P.H., is the founding principal of the HeartWork Group, a San Francisco based organizational development firm. She is a clinical psychologist, an organizational consultant, and the author of nine books, among them *Managing Organizational Change* and *Managing Personal Change.* Her education at U.C. Berkeley, the University of Michigan, and the Fielding Institute in organizational psychology, anthropology, and health management, combined with her corporate experience, bridges the gap between individual and organizational performance. In addition, she is a frequent speaker at corporate conferences on visionary leadership and organizational performance.

3   Using the *Strong Interest Inventory* and the *Myers-Briggs Type Indicator* Together in Career Counseling

Jean M. Kummerow, Ph.D., is a licensed consulting psychologist and principal of Jean Kummerow & Associates in St. Paul, Minnesota. She specializes in career counseling, management assessment and development, team building, and other organizational interventions through the applied use of psychology. While she uses a variety of psychological assessment tools in her work, she particularly enjoys the *Myers-Briggs Type Indicator* and the *Strong Interest Inventory* and trains professionals extensively on their use. She has written articles on team building, women's career development, and adult development and has developed training courses and other materials on type. She is co-author of *Introduction to Type in Organizations* and *LIFETypes*. She received her education from the University of Minnesota and Grinnell College.

4   Competency Profiling: A New Model for Career Counselors

Richard J. Mirabile, Ph.D., is currently president of Behavioral Systems Management Group, a human resources consulting firm in Half Moon Bay, California, specializing in management assessment, career management, and organizational effectiveness programs. Formerly he was vice president of program development for Ward Associates where he designed human resource programs, was an assistant professor in the Department of Supervision at Purdue University, and served as staffing and development manager for GTE Telephone Operations. Mirabile is the author of *Career Decisions: Strategies for Enrichment* as well as numerous articles in professional journals on the subject of human resource development and career management. He is currently completing a second book on career management systems in organizations.

5   The Realignment of Workers and Work in the 1990s

Andrea Saveri, M.A., is a researcher at the Institute for the Future in Menlo Park, California. Her research covers three areas: labor force trends, new information technologies, and health care. She evaluates the long-term effects of demographic shifts on the labor force, particularly how greater numbers of working women are affecting the workplace, employers, and the family structure. She also analyzes how new information technologies are changing business structures, education, and health care. Saveri holds academic degrees from U.C. Berkeley and Harvard University.

6   Meeting the Needs of the Multicultural Work Force

David C. Wigglesworth, Ph.D., is a human resource development professional and is president and prime consultant of D.C.W. Research Associates International in Foster City, California. He is a recognized authority on intercultural and international human resource development and was the recipient of ASTD's International Practitioner of the Year Award in 1988. He has published frequently in professional journals and is an invited presenter at national and international conferences.

7 Working Couples:
Finding a Balance Between Family and Career

Mark Guterman, M.A., is president of G & G Associates, a business aimed at teaching individuals and organizations the process of career growth. Guterman also teaches career development at JFK University, is a career counselor, and trains and consults for organizations in various aspects of career development. He is a member of the Bay Area Organization Development Network and the Career Planning and Adult Development Network, and is a frequent speaker for organizations and conferences throughout California. Guterman received his education from UCLA and Sonoma State University.